# REAL STORIES FROM A NUCLEAR SUBMARINER

*Once Upon a Time...*
*This Ain't No Bullshit*

## ALAN S. VOTTA

Copyrighted Material
REAL STORIES FROM A SUBMARINER:
Once Upon a Time/This Ain't No Bullshit

Copyright © 2021 by AV Publishing LLC

ALL RIGHTS RESERVED
No part of this publication may be reproduced, stored in a retrieval system or transmitted, in any form or by any means—electronic, mechanical, photocopying, recording or otherwise—without prior written permission from the publisher, except for the inclusion of brief quotations in a review.

For information about this title or to order other books and/or electronic media, contact the publisher:
AV Publishing LLC
1176 Tahiti Parkway
Sarasota, FL 34236
AV Publishers.com
508-221-8650

Library of Congress Control Number: 2021908379

ISBNs: 978-0-9889757-5-0 Print
978-0-9889757-6-7 eBook

Printed in the United States of America

Cover and Interior Design: 1106 Design

Publisher's Cataloging-In-Publication Data
(Prepared by The Donohue Group, Inc.)

Names: Votta, Alan S., author.
Title: Real stories from a nuclear submariner : once upon a time -- this ain't no bullshit / Alan S. Votta.
Description: Sarasota, FL : AV Publishing LLC, [2021]
Identifiers: ISBN 9780988975750 (print) | ISBN 9780988975767 (ebook)
Subjects: LCSH: Votta, Alan S. | Submariners--United States--Biography. | Nuclear submarines--United States. | LCGFT: Autobiographies.
Classification: LCC V63.V75 A3 2021 (print) | LCC V63.V75 (ebook) | DDC 359.93092--dc23

*Dedicated to all the United States Navy Silent Service Members who served before me, to those who continue to serve today, and to those who will follow.*

# Acknowledgments

Although my dedication for this book is to all submariners who served before me and to those who serve now, I also want to acknowledge the many *silent service* members who lost their lives aboard submarines, especially those who served on the *USS Thresher* SSN-593 and the *USS Scorpion* SSN-589. I would also like to acknowledge the 16,000 submariners who served in World War II, of whom 375 officers and 3,131 enlisted men were killed, who are now on watch on *eternal patrol* and reside in "Davy Jones' Locker." The United States Navy's submarine service suffered the highest casualty percentage of all American forces, losing one in five submarines over the course of World War II.

I wish to thank all of the friends and family members who have listened to my stories over the years and have found some interest, intrigue, honor, and humor in them. I hope that, by putting my stories together here, I have piqued their curiosity and given a more complete understanding of the mysterious world of the silent service and of the life I lived onboard the many subs on which I served. While writing this book, I was continuously amazed at how many more stories surfaced in my brain, beyond the ones that were my usual repertoire.

I also wish to thank the people who assisted by reading early drafts of the book and offering comments and suggestions—particularly dear friend Frank Forcelli, who, after reading an early draft, felt compelled to offer a rebuttal—in his own inimitable way. I'd also like to thank my cousin Joseph Piccolo, retired CIA Field Agent, who offered cogent remarks and agreed to write a testimonial, which appears on the cover of my book.

A special thanks goes to John Delzio, a family member on my wife's side, who strongly suggested I write this book. Thank you, John.

The book may be my words, but believe me when I say they would not make much sense without the endless and relentless editing by my editor-in-chief—my wife, Ann. Ann took my pile of incongruous words and turned them into intelligible paragraphs and pages resulting in the narrative and stories which follow. I wrote the entire manuscript in longhand on yellow legal pads, after which Ann entered it all, giving the book some much-needed structure.

And, lastly, to all my readers, I hope that I have given you more insight and a true picture of the building of a submarine and the day-to-day life onboard. And it is my sincere hope that I have conveyed the honor I feel in having served in the United States Navy as a Nuclear Submariner.

# Contents

Introduction   1

## Part One - My Early Days in the Navy   5

A. I Join Up   7
    1. Enlisting   7
    2. Off to Boot Camp   10
    3. Company 101   12

B. Training and Submarine School   17
    1. Key West, Florida   17
    2. New London, Connecticut   23
    3. Dam Neck, Virginia   28

C. Building Submarines   39
    1. Electric Boat General Dynamics   41
    2. Submarine Launch   56
    3. Around the Shipyard   72

## PART TWO - FIRST DAYS AT SEA · · · · · · · · · · 81

- A. Sea Trials · · · · · · · · · · · · · · · · · · · · · · · 83
  1. USS Thresher · · · · · · · · · · · · · · · · · · 87
  2. Missile Launch Testing · · · · · · · · · · · 88

- B. Post-Op Sea Trials · · · · · · · · · · · · · · · · · 95
  1. Welcome Home and Ceremony · · · · · 95
  2. LCU System (Life Change Unit System) · · 96

- C. Charleston, South Carolina · · · · · · · · · · 101
  1. My Arrival · · · · · · · · · · · · · · · · · · · 101
  2. The Strip · · · · · · · · · · · · · · · · · · · · 104
  3. Fleet Ballistic Missile Submarine Training Center · · · · · · · · · · · · · · · · 111

## PART THREE - FIRST PATROL · · · · · · · · · · · 115

- A. Rota, Spain · · · · · · · · · · · · · · · · · · · · · 117
- B. Preparations for Patrol · · · · · · · · · · · · · 127
- C. Life Onboard · · · · · · · · · · · · · · · · · · · 131
- D. Other Subs and Commands · · · · · · · · · 157

## PART FOUR - PHASE TWO OF MY NAVAL CAREER · · 169

- A. Becoming a Naval Instructor · · · · · · · · 171
  1. Naval Instructor Training School, Norfolk, Virginia · · · · · · · · · · · · · · 171

Contents

   2. Back to Charleston, South Carolina, and
       FBMSTC     176

B. Real Life as a Submariner     185
   1. Personal Life     185
   2. A Major Decision     187

C. Civilian Life     203

# Part Five - Final Stories     209

A. *USS Thresher* SSN-593     213
B. The *Hunley*     217
C. Strange Occurrences or Stranger Encounters     219
D. A Submarine Sailor Walked into a Bar…     223

About the Author     227

# INTRODUCTION

For you lucky bastards who have picked up this book to read, you are in for a treat. Don't look for a message, guidance, or great enlightenment in the pages that follow. This isn't that, folks. But if you'd like an honest look at the building of the earliest nuclear submarines in the United States in the 1960s, you will enjoy my stories.

The title of this book is a two-parter—*Real Stories from a Nuclear Submariner* and *Once Upon a Time…. This Ain't No Bullshit*. There is a reason for that, which I will explain later, and it has to do with how stories are told onboard a submarine in the Navy. The book is a gathering of the thoughts and experiences I had while being immersed (or better yet, being a victim of total immersion) into the United States Navy Submarine Service. The language may be a little salty from time to time, but it is reality. Every soul who ever joined any military service has a *story* of just how it became his or her life's choice. This is mine.

Mine was simple. It all started when the love of my life, my high school sweetheart, dumped me when we came back home for Christmas vacation after our first semester at college. I didn't handle that very well. I ultimately left college and bounced around for a short while, trying to gain some direction and purpose. A friend from college had joined the Navy after high school and served his time. When I met him, I noticed how mature he seemed. I thought, "Maybe the Navy could help me find a new path forward." My plan of action was set in motion. Plus, my older brother had completed a stint in the Navy as well, and he had shared many of his sea stories with me. My original thought had been to join the French Foreign Legion, only to find out that it (unfortunately for me) had been disbanded many years before.

What follows here are my various experiences: some crazy, some tragic, some hilarious, some courageous, but most of them exhilarating. This is what happened to me during my twenty-four-year career in the United States Nuclear Submarine Navy. The timeframe is 1962 to 1986.

This isn't another *Red October* or other popular rendition of life on a submarine but rather, a compilation of the real day-to-day happenings of an enlisted man who rose to the rank of Chief.

As I look back over my Naval career and of the many exploits that I was part of, it is mind-blowing to think of it all, particularly the Nuclear Power Program. I was part of the integral oversight of the building of nuclear power submarines. All of my comrades and I were privileged and blessed to be chosen to partake in that grand adventure. I firmly believe that

# Introduction

we were a genuine example of the United States of America's finest young men, who were willing to sacrifice their lives each and every day. They were and are "a true cut above" and "made of the right stuff."

The American public had no idea why they were breathing free and pursuing dreams that were protected at all times by our deterrent nuclear Submarine Navy. Our enemies never knew where our deterrent silent service submarines were. It was *Star Wars* of sorts, but underwater and completely REAL. The same holds true for today.

I am very proud of my service, and I savor every minute of my experience during those years. I hope you enjoy some of my *Real Stories* and adventures.

# Part One

# My Early Days in the Navy

# A. I Join Up

## 1. Enlisting

I was all set to join the Navy. The day I went to the recruiting station in my hometown of Yonkers, New York, I somehow had a change of heart and decided on impulse to join—the Marines! At the office there were many recruiters representing all of the branches of the United States services. I began talking to other potential recruits. I went there cold turkey, with no appointment. After a bit of voyeurism and eavesdropping with the Marine recruits, a Navy recruiter spotted me and asked if he could help. He explained that they all worked together. He told me he could administer a basic recruitment written test and we could go from there—whichever direction I would choose to go. I took the test. By this time, I had heard and witnessed enough to rule out the Marines.

The Navy recruiter scored my test and told me that my results were such that he could recommend me for something special. A new adventure was available to me…and that was the Nuclear Submarine Navy! I would be in on the ground floor of a grand and brand-new adventure. I would also receive plenty of schooling, which would enhance my future in all ways. I immediately thought of all the possible submerged time I might experience—time for me to heal my love, or lack-of-love, wounds.

I committed to the United States Navy, and I felt really good about it. Besides, having listened to the Jarheads (Marines) talking, I realized that I didn't want to carry a knife between my teeth, bare-chested, carrying my gun and rushing over all manner of obstacles to thrash and kill the enemy—the predominant image in my mind after my discussion with the Marine recruits. Plus, the coffee the Navy recruiter was filling me with was pretty damn good and strong!

I waited for induction day. I finally got my notice for a full physical and additional written tests. Next stop was Whitehall Street, downtown Manhattan in New York City. That day arrived, and I drove down and, not without difficulty, found a parking space and entered the hallowed halls where millions of World War I, World War II, Korean, and now the Vietnam-era men had gone before me. I found myself among hundreds of bodies—hundreds of scared souls trying to figure out how we got to this point in our lives.

Eventually, every one of us, bare-ass naked, were being poked and prodded, and a complete record of everything about our physical and mental condition from the examiners' written reports was developed. We were a sorry-looking group of every size, shape, and dimension. Every color of the rainbow was represented, along with the variations of male

## My Early Days in the Navy

genitalia. Scary to say the least. We couldn't help but peek to compare and either envy or feel sorry for some. I am so glad I am heterosexual!

Now to the part that got me into the Nuclear Submarine Navy—aptitude testing. We were seated at small desks with a partition separating each desk. Test after test came at us, and, honestly, I found it all fairly easy. A guy to my right leaned around the partition and said to me, "9 times 9?" I was sure he was indicating how easy the test was, so I said, "102." He tilted toward me and continued to ask questions, seemingly mocking the test, so I continued to give him absurd answers. However, when the testing was over, he came to me and thanked me for helping him through the exam. I almost croaked. I never learned what happened to him.

After the day was done, if you made it and were successful with everything, you were told that you would receive a letter in the mail indicating your day of departure to Boot Camp. I returned to my parked car (my dad's car) only to find a $30 parking ticket on the windshield. I have ignored that sucker to this date and wonder if I may still get a letter in the mail requesting a $10,000 remittance after all of the interest is compounded. Nothing yet.

Finally, the letter arrived. I went back to Whitehall Street, with just the clothes on my back, and off we all went—the Marines to Paris Island, Air Force to Texas, and we, the Navy-types, were off to the lovely Great Lakes Naval Training Facility.

## 2. Off to Boot Camp

And then the fun began. We traveled by rail—not in first class or business class, of course. Recruits travel on what is termed the *milk route,* which necessitates frequent and quick stops. Every time we looked out the window, the ground seemed to be moving in a different direction. We literally traveled from New Jersey in a saw-toothed up-and-down route all the way—government special rate—to the Great Lakes. We accumulated over a thousand miles of travel that should have been around eight hundred miles.

We finally made it, and we were then loaded onto buses to the Great Lakes Naval Recruit Training Station. This was Camp Moffett, an old red-brick building looking more like a state mental hospital than the *resort* we were expecting. We were herded into a building, and since it was the middle of February, there was plenty of snow piled up. When we entered the building, we had to traverse icy steps down into the building. At the end of training, I returned to that building. With the snow and ice gone, I realized that there were steps going up that were previously hidden by the quantity of snow on the ground.

We grabbed our assigned bunk, and after a few personal details were settled, we all crashed for some much-needed sleep. Sometime later, while in a very deep sleep, I heard an earth-shattering noise. It startled the hell out of me! Let's call it what it was—frightening beyond compare. The recruits who had been there longer than we *newbies* had the joy of waking up the so-called new blood, or the new recruits. We soon learned

## My Early Days in the Navy

that this was the manner in which we were to be awakened each day. Imagine a coke bottle inside of an old-time corrugated steel garbage can being spun around the interior of the garbage can, hitting all of the ribs. The noise was deafening, overwhelming, and disorienting, and we newbies were scared shitless—much to the delight of the more senior recruits. Mind you, this was at 4 a.m. and the temperature outside was no higher than 10 degrees.

We were instructed to "shit, shower, and shave," utilizing the small bag of essentials issued to us, and then we were off to breakfast. This was followed by my first encounter with the infamous breakfast delight called *shit-on-a-shingle*—that is, chipped beef in a heavy gravy (like wallpaper paste) placed over the top of dry toast. That dish is disgusting, and it causes me to cringe just to think of it after all these many years.

The next step was uniform fitting, which included all of the items to complete our new wardrobe. Most of these new clothes were nowhere near a custom fit. They were what they were, and we had to make do with what we got.

So began my Navy career. And so did the experiences that led to my *stories,* which I share with you now. However, before I get into the stories, I guess it is time to explain the subtitle of the book, *Once Upon a Time… This Ain't No Bullshit.*

One can only imagine that, when you have so many talented and colorful men brought together for a very complicated and challenging adventure, there will, consequently, be very interesting and sometimes mind-boggling topics/stories told. After a while you become aware of certain trends and/or characteristics in each story told by one of your fellow crew members. Now here is the Rosetta Stone of a submariner's stories. When a story starts with "Once Upon a Time…" everyone quickly judges the story as a total fabrication, and you should take every word with a grain of salt. *However,* if, or when, your fellow submariner starts out by saying, "This ain't no bullshit…," you can bet your bottom dollar this story is—absolutely, beyond any doubt—a story based on facts, with witnesses!

As I begin my storytelling, I will leave it up to you, but from my perspective, *all* of my stories come under the latter heading.

## 3. Company 101

Now back to my first days as a Navy recruit.

This was also the big day that we picked up our Company Commander—a Chief or a First-Class Petty Officer who would form our group into a company. We became Company 101, led by Chief Boilerman James L. Roddy. I will tell you here and now, Chief Roddy was a true professional, and he guided us to become a very successful boot camp company, garnering a great many prestigious achievements, signified by the number of flags accumulated in competitions against other companies of recruits. As Chief Roddy introduced himself to us, I liked him instantly. This adventure continued with a great leader, who guided us all the way through training.

In record time, we were shaped up into a company made up of two platoons consisting of a total of six squads. Chief Roddy picked a Recruit Petty Officer Chief to lead the entire company. He asked the group if anybody had any background

## My Early Days in the Navy

in military organizations. One gentleman was a military school graduate. Voila. He now became our RPOC. Initially, I became the Master-at-Arms, the guy who was the enforcer. I also chose a person to be our Company Clerk, who took on administrative responsibilities.

We marched our fool heads off. But the new RPOC was not working out too well. He looked the part, but the role was not his forte. So, in the middle of nowhere, Chief Roddy relieved him of his duties, stripped him of the status symbol of the RPOC—a webbed belt and sword—handed them to me, and said, "I should have chosen you in the first place." So, I, Alan Stephen Votta, was now the new RPOC. With NO background or formal training, I was to march the entire company through hazards, brooks, streams, and busy streets back to our barracks—with snow on the ground to add a little flavor to the mix! All of a sudden, I was in the hot seat. I pulled all that I needed completely out of my ass and got our company back safely and soundly. As time went on, it all got better and better, and I was happy to be in the position I was in.

### Story: Disaster Turned to Triumph

A little hiccup arose. One of my squad leaders, by the name of Graziano, decided to become a thorn in my side. His attitude toward me messed with the overall morale of the group and undermined my ability to lead. It seems he supported the previous RPOC, and he determined I was the real problem and that I was not his friend. Mr. Graziano was built like a fireplug, with muscle to spare and a big fat mouth, which could be very intimidating.

Time went on, and Graziano soon became a real problem for me, and I knew I had to deal with the situation. I was certain any encounter would be physical—no words or diplomacy were going to be enough. This pain-in-my-ass predicament came to a head in the barracks in front of the entire company. We finally managed to get into a shouting match, and I invited this son-of-a-bitch to follow me into a nearby empty barrack. I led the way, and I was thinking that I would be lucky to come out of this alive. We wound up *mano a mano*—hand-to-hand, one on one. We stared. And we shared some choice words. I calculated that I had to strike first—and so I did! I punched him square on the left side of his face. He was completely stunned. His reaction was to grab me in a bear hug. I thought that, very soon, I would be in two pieces. He stayed frozen with his arms around me…bleeding. Finally speaking, he said to me, "I never thought you would do it—hit me." He repeated those words over and over again.

When he let go of me, I didn't know what to expect. What Graziano did completely stymied me. He walked back toward our barrack and returned to where all of the troops were standing by. Since he entered long before me and he was bloodied, I'm sure the rest of the men thought that I must be lying dead in the other building. When I walked in, completely unscathed, there was a deafening silence. The troops could not figure out what had just happened. The silence was broken when Graziano started screaming out to everyone, telling them all that "If anybody ever gives RPOC Alan Votta a hard time,

## My Early Days in the Navy

I personally will kick your ass." I was befuddled, but quite relieved, at the outcome. From that day on, Graziano became my biggest supporter and enforcer, and all was peaceful and positive in our little universe.

—⚜—

The overall comradeship of the entire company was boosted immensely. So much so, that we accrued more flags (trophies) than any other company before us. When Company 101 graduated, we achieved the designation *Color Company*—the best of the best, out of the multitude of companies competing.

And I was singled out by being presented our Company Flag (Company 101), which was signed by every member of my company. And the biggest signature was that of our Company Commander, Chief Boilerman James L. Roddy. He also wrote some words of praise and ended his efforts by adding that he hoped my United States Navy Service would be marked by "Fair winds and smooth sailing." And to this day, I share those words with many friends and family, just as I am wishing all of my readers, "Fair winds and smooth sailing."

Now for a little sidebar. It seems that Admiral Rickover (the Father of the Nuclear Submarine Navy) presented every new submarine commanding officer with a brass paperweight—a 3-inch by 4-inch piece depicting a 3D submarine amidst 3D waves with the words "Fair winds and smooth sailing" written on the bottom. Thus, my flag with those very words took on even a stronger meaning for me.

*Real Stories from a Nuclear Submariner*

How about a little more icing on this cake? Years later, I became a proud owner of one of those paperweights. A foundry man in Electric Boat General Dynamics, who cast the paperweights for Admiral Rickover, was a friend of mine. Although he worked for twenty-five years in the shipyard, he had never been aboard a submarine. After I took him and his son on a tour of a submarine at Sub Base New London, he presented me with one of the paperweights. He said the tour on the sub was "the highlight of their lives." The paperweight was his way of saying thank you.

# B. Training and Submarine School

## 1. Key West, Florida

Back to my training. As recruit graduates, before heading to our first duty stations, we were headed out to our respective homes all over the USA to celebrate our new status and show off our uniforms. We also wanted to show off by telling our sea stories, which became slightly exaggerated, or, let's say, totally contrived, since we had not been out to sea yet!

Instead of being on my way to a submarine, my path became filled with school after school to prepare for a first day on any submarine. The first school I was assigned to was in Key West, Florida—long before the entire cruise-ship invasion, for electronics and electricity training. (Matter of fact, today the cruise ships all moor where the old Navy Base was located.) I loved the island back then, and I would usually stay in Key West on weekends off, while others rushed up the highway to Miami and Fort Lauderdale. The school and barracks (no a/c then, by the way) were actually a number of schools brought together for the many sailors from around the fleet on this relatively small island of Key West.

## Story: Keeping Cool

On my first night in my new barracks (no a/c—but numerous overhead fans) I woke up to a disturbance and witnessed an old drunken sailor taking the mattresses off of the unoccupied bunks. After many trips, he managed to cover the floor of the gang shower area with said mattresses. When he was finished with his mosaic of mattresses, he turned on all of the cold-water taps and lay down to a soggy "water/conditioned" deep sleep, snoring to beat the band. This character was the first of many Navy Old Salts (sailors who drank *evil spirits* to excess because they had a lot of time on their hands and not much else to do), whom I would encounter over the years.

—⚓—

I was not a teetotaler, and I drank my share of beer, but I had to realize that being in Key West was another test of my character. On my first night out on the town in downtown Key West, I discovered, almost tragically, how dangerous Key West could be. As I crossed the street going from one bar to the next, I looked and checked for traffic to my left, and it was clear. I stepped out onto the road, and a car came to a screeching halt, with its bumper almost touching my knee. That is how I was made aware of the fact that Main Street/Duval Street in downtown Key West was a one-way street! Looking right

## My Early Days in the Navy

and left took on a new meaning to me. I survived. During that time, I first tasted and joyfully consumed turtle burgers, langoustine, and REAL key lime pie—not the crap put on menus all over the U.S. today.

### Story: A Serendipitous Encounter

This is a rather longish story that was brought to my mind recently, which sparked a long-forgotten memory and an unforeseen incident I had while I was thumbing my way back to Key West after a lackluster visit to Miami. I mentioned before that I usually stayed in Key West when I had time off, but one weekend, I was fortunate enough to get a ride from Key West to Miami. I was on my own, and with no real plan or purpose, I poked around until I came upon a theater presenting the mega grand opening of the movie *Cleopatra*. After seeing the long line and being shocked at the $5 ticket price, I quickly lost interest. (It took me ten years to finally see that movie, and I was glad that I did not waste $5, because I thought it was all cleavage and no plot! I ultimately saw it on a luxury billion-dollar submarine, as I enjoyed free popcorn and soft serve ice cream at 300 feet under the Atlantic Ocean.)

As I became disenchanted with South Beach, Miami, I decided to head to the mainland and further explore the old downtown real Miami—not the tourist trap at the beach. As I was content walking on the causeway connecting the island with the mainland, a car pulled up alongside me, and the driver said to me, "You have the look of a man trying to get downtown and off this godforsaken island!" I responded,

"You are right!" He and his wife offered me a ride, and I gladly accepted. When we arrived downtown, the Reverend Ray Sonta and his wife, Patricia, parked the car, and we wound up having a tremendous conversation. They were both missionaries and were running a mission in one of the Latin American countries. After a lengthy discussion, they gave me their contact information and told me that if, after my Navy stint, I wanted some additional adventure, I should reconnect with them and become part of their great mission. I often wonder about Rev. Ray and his charming wife.

The day was wearing on, and I was convinced that Miami really was not my cup of tea. All I wanted at that point was to get back to Key West, where I should have stayed in the first place. Heading in the direction of Key West, I managed to get a ride or two across the first causeway, and I wondered how long it would take before I would secure a ride all the way to Key West.

The first island one comes to after leaving the continental USA is Key Largo. Back in the day, that island was like Gilligan's Island…relatively calm, quiet, and beautiful, and not overrun with tourists. I then started realizing that this could be a rather long and tedious journey. I had not considered the road would be so desolate; it was getting dark, and I was getting tired. Off in the distance, I saw some signs of human activity, but as I approached, I became leery of knocking on doors, so instead, I decided to crawl into a derelict car nearby and try to get some sleep. I thought that I could get refreshed and resume my travel adventure thereafter. I had plenty of time since it was Saturday evening, and my deadline to get back

## My Early Days in the Navy

on base was Monday morning. As hard as I tried, I could not relax and fall off to sleep. I finally decided to get back on old Route 1 and continue my journey on foot...come what may.

A couple of hours later—a miracle was about to happen! Out of the darkness, a car came heading in the proper direction. I stood in the road, and, as the car approached, I realized that the driver might think that I was some kind of lunatic and that he would race right by me. Instead, the car slowed down and stopped. I approached the driver's window, and an exhausted and very tired-looking gentleman asked me where I was going. He then asked me if I had a driver's license. The answer, of course, was "Yes!" He said that if I would drive the car, I could drive to exactly where I had to be in Key West, and by then he would be rested enough to drive himself back up Route 1 to Boca Chica—the island just north of Key West—which was his ultimate destination. He informed me that he had just undergone an operation (purpose unknown) in Chicago, Illinois, and instead of recovering there, he became impatient to get back to Boca Chica, and he set out to drive all the way there.

He told me that his name was Mel Fisher. That name rang a bell with me. After he mentioned that he was also a treasure hunter, I instantly recognized his name. He was the man currently trying to find the wreck of the Spanish Galleon called the *Atocha*, which was allegedly filled with gold and artifacts.

As coincidence would have it, I had recently read an extensive article about Mr. Fisher. At the end of the article, there was an offer to buy shares in his exploration endeavor. Sure wish I had bought some of those shares! As I got behind the wheel and before he dozed off, we had a great chitchat about all of that. Soon after, he just passed out from exhaustion.

When we arrived in Key West, I parked near the entrance to the Navy Annex Base and quickly and quietly decided to let Mr. Fisher sleep on, and I gratefully did the same. When he finally awoke, he was in a much better and rejuvenated state of mind and body, and we talked on for about another hour plus. Mr. Fisher invited me to his museum and gift shop on Boca Chica, and he told me that if I ever wanted to, after my Navy career was over, I could come and work for him.

I ultimately did visit his museum, and he treated me extremely well. He told me that if it hadn't been for me, he probably would have had a major car wreck and possibly killed himself, and that I was an angel sent by God to save his stubborn butt. He treated me royally, and I became part of the family. I met his son and daughter-in-law, who eventually died in a terrible accident when the sleeping barge capsized and trapped the young couple. They, along with a third person…a diver…drowned.

Eventually, my next assignment was upon me, and I was on my way to United States Navy Submarine School in New London, Connecticut. Sad to say, I never had any further contact with Mel Fisher and his future mega discovery of the *Atocha* and the treasure of immense magnitude.

—⚓—

On my last visit to Key West three or four years ago, I was a tourist on a cruise ship, and I visited the Mel Fisher Museum

## My Early Days in the Navy

(at its new location in Key West rather than in Boca Chica) once again. It vividly brought back all of these memories, but I soon realized that I could not wait to get out of the tourist zoo that Key West has become. It kind of ruined all of my fond memories of such a special place.

When I was there in the '60s, I felt like it was a tropical wonderland with an exotic atmosphere and personality. No wonder it became the home and playground of writer Ernest Hemingway and noted wildlife artist James Audubon. Now, it is like a tacky, tainted, contrived island of tourist mediocrity and eyesores. Sorry, Key West lovers. Nothing stays the same, and we live in a world where special and one-of-a kind places get ruined with the invasion of the cruise-ship industry. My opinion anyway.

Key West became a memory, as after graduation from electronic and electricity school, I was on my way to United States Submarine School in New London, Connecticut—the real biggie in a Navy career. I was stoked.

## 2. New London, Connecticut

When I arrived at New London, I almost wet my pants because I was so proud to be a part of this truly special group of men on the face of the Earth. Talk about tradition, history, and aura of magnificence. Here I was, Alan Stephen Votta, among the best of the best, and I would have to work my ass off to achieve and continue to be good enough to be part of this "Special World of Special Men," that is, the extremely complex world of nuclear submarines of the United States Nuclear Submarine Navy.

## Story: An Interesting Bet

I burned the midnight oil studying to be the best prepared that I could possibly become. And it all paid off. I graduated at the top of my class. One glitch occurred, however. I failed a strategic written test, and I was devastated, to say the least. I sought to take a re-test. I was so adamant about being allowed to re-take the test that I told the higher-ups I would make a bet with them. I bet I could score what you call a "Chinese 100%" on the test if I were allowed to take it again. That meant that I would make sure I would purposely get every question *wrong!* That proposal got the entire office of instructors looking at me with quizzical looks and a bunch of wry smiles. The challenge was accepted, and I and my big fat mouth were either going to make it, or break me. And I had to take the test right there in the instructors' office!

I sat down, and I was presented with a new test created for this area. And I was going to be the virgin or guinea pig. How do you think I did? Well, I got my Chinese 100%. Frankly, I wasn't so sure about it when I handed in my test booklet—but I did it! Thankfully, the rest of my school tenure contained no more such drama.

---

## The Tank

The day that we all were kinda, sorta, very worried about, came. We had to go to *the tank*. On the lower base sat a circular thirty-foot-around and 100-foot-tall structure. It

## My Early Days in the Navy

was an ominous edifice, and what makes it really scary to every submarine school student is the test of frightening proportions that takes place in there and must be passed. At two levels, there is a lockout chamber. It is 100 feet to the top at ground level. The first lockout is at ground level and then another at 50 feet. The water pressure at 100 feet is substantial, so instructors pack eight sub students at a time into the lockout chamber at ground level and fill the chamber to above the hatch to enter the tank. First, after flooding the water in, the air space in the chamber had to be pressurized, which was from about our shoulders up. Flooding the chamber was enough to have one or two students panic. A quick reversal of chamber activity allowed those poor souls out, and they exited the submarine community, never to be seen again. Some men never showed panic until the air pressure was applied. The noise of the equalizing air could be frightening in itself. That noise of screaming air eliminated another one or two.

Now let's get back to the intended purpose of the tank. If a sub sinks at a reasonable depth, the sub has a lockout chamber built into the submarine design to facilitate escape from a sunken sub. So, back at the lockout chamber on lower base, the water level was up to shoulder level. Now apply the high pressure to equalize with the water pressure at 100 feet below the surface of the water above. When you reach that, you're in tight quarters in a steel bubble chamber with water up to your shoulders, and you are crammed in this chamber with six to eight fellow novices. Then you hear a blood-curdling noise level of the air entering. OK. Ready?

The massive fucking door now can be opened to allow us to get out. That's a misnomer. At this point, the only way you are getting out is to duck down and enter the tank (with no air tanks or external devices). You place your arms and hands straight up—so you don't hit any floating debris on the surface of the water—and you ascend at a rapid rate because of the air compressed in your lungs. That air has to be allowed out of your lungs. So, each of us has to continuously exhale, shouting "Ho! Ho! Ho!" ensuring a constant flow of air out of your lungs, or you can damage your lungs, or worse, rupture your air passages permanently. To ensure this does not happen, there are dive instructors with breathing apparatus at intervals every twenty feet. If they see a student in trouble and not exhaling adequately, they will pop him in the belly to force the air out of his lungs. And if a student is in total distress, dive instructors will take charge, go into lifesaver mode, and save the student from any damage. When this happens, one or two students decide that volunteering for submarines is not really their cup of tea, and they wind up with orders to the surface craft part of the U.S. Navy.

This tank experience reoccurs in a submariner's life on a yearly basis. Oh, and by the way, I passed with flying colors—along with many others. Six of the men failed, with no follow-up attempts possible. The first result could never be changed.

## *Story: Scavenger Hunt*

On the lighter side, following that horrific experience, about six or seven of us wound up going on a scavenger hunt out in

## My Early Days in the Navy

the civilian world to celebrate. The hunt we planned was to go hopscotch all over Mystic, Connecticut, and the object was to put a sandwich together, picking up one ingredient at a time and hopefully having great conversations along the way and making lots of new friends. We had a great time, and the civilians we encountered enjoyed our pursuit as well. New friendships were made, and the interest in our submarine connection grew.

However, we overloaded our ass at one particular house, and one of our gang decided to bullshit about his submarine experience—of which he had zero onboard time. All of the onboard time we ever really had was that we went out to sea on the *USS Conger* 477 for a day—one day! We dove one time, and, thankfully, we surfaced one time, and that was it. The bullshit got really heavy, and our friend exaggerated with one story after another. The man of the house seemed content to listen, and he asked some very good questions. After he had been entertained enough, he politely told us he was also a submariner and had been in for twenty-five years—a World War II submarine survivor and the Chief of the Boat currently onboard the *USS Nautilus* SS 571, the first nuclear submarine ever built. The Chief of the Boat is the most prestigious honor for an enlisted man to achieve onboard a submarine. He allowed us to be sufficiently embarrassed and had a good laugh at our expense, justifiably so, and he invited us to visit whenever we could.

We wore out our welcome for now at the Submarine School Command, however, a whole bunch of potential submariners were steps closer to our main objective—the seemingly ever-elusive set of orders to our respective submarines.

## 3. Dam Neck, Virginia

A necessary delay once again until getting onboard a sub was our attendance at still another school. This one was in Dam Neck, Virginia. It was a Polaris Missile Launcher School. I also must mention the numerous psychological evaluations a submarine student is subjected to. After all, the Navy can't afford to spend all of this money on educating men who can't take the rigors of solitary, complex, and desolate submarine life.

I was faced with a slightly different kind of exam one day. I had a so-called hearing test scheduled, however, the location for that test was somewhat peculiar. I went to a large room. This rather large room had thousands of long sound-absorbing baffles around it—so many, that when you spoke, you had to talk directly at the person in front of you, whom you could barely hear because of those absorbing baffles. In the middle of this huge area was a strange, rather thick-walled room approximately 10' × 10' × 10'. The walls and door of this structure were at least one foot thick. I was instructed to sit inside, and put the earphones on, and listen to the audio directions. The door of pure doom was laboriously closed, and there I sat in TOTAL SILENCE. Even my thoughts were being absorbed away from me! That is pure exaggeration on my part. I don't want to turn this into a science-fiction thriller.

OK, the instructions I received over the headset guided me through the entire hearing test. I thought, however, that it was rather odd that there were people always staring at me through thick-glassed portholes and taking notes. At the end of the test, I was finally informed of the dual purpose of this so-called hearing test. I made sense of it all then. The thick-walled compartment was testing for claustrophobia, which was the main objective, with the hearing test secondary. I was told that some students could not last in the chamber of doom for a whole minute. After that test, another submarine candidate was gone—once again, to become a surface sailor. We affectionately called them "skimmers," or, worse yet, "targets," meaning they were very visible on the surface.

## *Story: Trip Home to Yonkers, New York*

Let's take a pause and a deep breath. I need to go to the lighter side again. During my period in New London Sub Base and then at Dam Neck, I was allowed numerous trips back to my hometown of Yonkers, New York. Many of those trips were noteworthy. With very little money available, one always had to use one's imagination. In New London and in Dam Neck, to make a little extra money, a friend of mine and I went to a pawnshop and bought a portable Singer sewing machine. Ah! You wonder why? I'll tell you why. At this point in our journey to become submariners, many sailors were earning promotions. That meant new insignias had to be sewn onto their uniforms, replacing the previous rank, and sometimes a little alteration was needed as well. Our creative operation continued for a significant amount of time, until the base alteration shop had us shut down! Oh, well—it was great while it lasted.

Now with this extra money, we could get to New York City and still have money to enjoy our visits. To save even more money, my main objective was to get to the underside of the George Washington Bridge. Fact is, it had been used by servicemen who congregated there ever since the bridge was built, in order to be picked up by well-meaning people who gave rides to those service members heading north on the West Side Drive. I think that tradition has died in recent years.

Here I was standing under the G.W. Bridge, and out of nowhere, a school bus (quite illegal on this road) pulled up. I was the only one there, so, of course, since I liked the look of this obviously illegal adventure, I stepped onboard. I couldn't believe what I saw in that vehicle—a stereo system, a home gas heater and tank, and a small fridge. I soon learned that, back in the day, since the driver had been an independent school bus driver for a private school in New York City, all this was legal and acceptable. We were on our way. I explained that he could drop me off as far north as he was going. But then he reached into the fridge, and we started drinking Schaefer beer. After a lot of good-to-great bullshit storytelling, it became obvious that we were getting shit-faced. In time, this school bus, with Steve Montone at the wheel and Alan Votta, his passenger, were parked in front of 177 Orchard Street, Yonkers, New York. Yes, my home!

As if on cue, my dad came out of the house to walk the family dog, and he was startled to see a school bus blocking the street. When the door to the bus opened, his inebriated son introduced him to Steve Montone, who was equally brewed up. I exited the bus, and Steve yelled out to my dad, "You got one

## My Early Days in the Navy

hell of a great fucking son!" With no further words spoken, off drove Steve Montone down the street, headed back to the city—lights flashing and horns blaring, and with a mighty "Hi Ho Silver," Steve Montone was a blur on the horizon.

—⁂—

Are you up for one more? Who gives a shit? I am going to tell it no matter what you think! Besides, if you are still reading this drivel, your life ain't worth much, and you need a diversion.

### *Story: Another Trip Back Home*

Here we go. Sometime later after that first experience of getting back home, I was in New York City again trying to get to Yonkers, and I had $2 to my name. So, as I had done in the past, I walked to the West Side Drive and hoofed it to the G.W. Bridge. That day, I decided to wave down a cabbie, and I told him to proceed to the West Side Drive and up the West Side Drive for as far as $2 would take me. Money is money, and I guess he didn't give a shit, and off we went. He spotted the bag I was carrying and asked about the imprint on it—Submarine Base New London. I explained a little bit more, and he then understood that I was in the Navy. I soon realized that he had some kind of problem that he was dealing with that involved the U.S. Navy. He told me that his son recently joined the Navy, and he (the father) was very distraught about that. I asked him to please explain, and he revealed a deep worry. "Because," he said, "I think my son is gay." That got my attention. How did he ascertain that gem of knowledge? It seems that his son was becoming a corpsman—a male medical nurse—in the Navy. And because of an affectionate term planted on corpsmen—that is, *pecker checkers*—his dad was allowing his imagination to go totally out of control, and thus, his assumption that his son was gay. Don't forget. This was the early 1960s.

I poured it on. I told him that the corpsmen were the most respected and admired people in the Navy. Without guns issued, they sometimes would have to dodge bullets. They were recognized by an emblem of a white circle with a red cross prominently in the middle—they were targets of the enemy! And in the field, they make life-threatening bold decisions that many times saved the lives of fellow sailors and Marines.

I further explained that my Uncle Eddie was an Army Medic during World War II (also affectionately nicknamed pecker-checker) and he became a hero over and over again. I also made him aware that my uncle carried a German Luger and an Italian Berretta—not so legal, but among many, a common practice. My uncle had to use these weapons from time to time to literally save his ass and the wounded he was caring for.

Back to my cabbie. I glanced at the meter and realized that the $2 mark had passed and so had the G.W. Bridge drop-off point. The cabbie's name was Richard Powers. We talked and talked and talked, and, before either of us knew it, because I had given him my home address and I unconsciously kept adding driving directions, we were at my front door at 177 Orchard Street, Yonkers, New York. He parked the cab, and he got out. He put his arms around me and thanked me profusely

## My Early Days in the Navy

for educating him and restoring the loving pride he had for his son, the pecker checker, as he drove off with tears in his eyes, never having taken a dime from me.

Update—update—update. Four years later, Mr. Powers tracked me down. He came to my house and explained to my parents who he was and that he wanted to contact me. We connected a month later, and we met in New York City at a restaurant called the Mayflower. We greeted one another with warm hugs and handshakes. With him was his son, the pecker checker, quite a fine gentleman. Eventually he showed me a picture of his wife and baby girl. "Not bad for a pecker checker," I thought. We had a good time together. Upon departing, Mr. Powers asked me about the restaurant, and I knew where he was heading. Just about every one of the patrons at the bar and in the dining area was obviously gay. He looked at me and laughed, as did I. His son had no clue as to why it was so extremely funny to us.

—ᴍ—

### Old Salts and Young Studs

Didn't I get diverted for a while! Back to Dam Neck, Virginia. Our class convened, and the handful of us (who were still shitting green and wet behind the ears)—were literally thrust into a group of ancient submarine types. So *salty* were they— the decorated World War II conventional submarine war heroes with medals and decorations to support them. They automatically gained our full respect and admiration. When they talked, it was like another language to us, and when they laughed, it was infectious. At that time, we were all a strategic part of building the Nuclear Power Submarine Division, which required forceful leadership to build capable and cohesive crews with an unyielding sense of purpose and desire. These guys experienced real combat with real consequences. In other words, all of the young brainiacs needed father figures to make everything work efficiently. We idolized them and stayed low key in their presence, even though we were all in the same school and classrooms. We were the *young studs*, and they were the *old salts*.

From the start, we, the young studs, had a special purpose. These old fuds had some difficulty being back in a classroom. For most of them, it had been many years since their last experience in that kind of environment. Since our subject matter was TOP SECRET, that meant all of our books and papers had to be locked up in our top-secret individual safe/lockers. The old salts had difficulty with the confusing combination-lock directions! So, we young studs took on the responsibility of opening their lockers. So much for Top Secret!

Lunch breaks were very interesting. We young studs went to the chow hall to eat some real food. The old salts went to the service clubs to have some grownup beverages, otherwise known as *liquid lunch*. Upon returning back to the classroom, the atmosphere was very animated and humorous—serious schooling going on there!

By the way, all of our classes were held from 4 p.m. to 12 midnight. One night during an extended break, a couple of the old salts disappeared. Aware that all of the clubs onboard

## My Early Days in the Navy

the base were closed, they knew there was no chance of running for a quick adult beverage or two. When these characters reappeared, they obviously had managed to have a drink or more. These old originals had found some warm beer in the car. They tied the beer to the bumper of the car and raced around the base and cooled the beer off enough, so that they could consume it more enjoyably.

You must try to imagine sitting amongst history. My youthful group and I were among men who had made war patrols onboard conventional submarines; some had even served on subs that were *depth charged*. This was not like the movies. This was real life—with a real enemy and real explosive charges trying to kill you and all your mates. The drinking became a non-problem. What these guys could do with a couple of brews under their belt was far greater than many stone-sober men in any and all situations.

### *Story: Some Don't Make It*

School went on, and there was a guy in our class who was trying to convert from the surface Navy to Submarines to reap the better pay that we automatically earned by being in a hazardous line of work. Thus, we all would be given hazardous-duty pay in addition to our regular pay, which was a nice chunk of change. This guy was having difficulty keeping up with the subject matter. Because he was trying so hard and for the right reasons—that is, earn more money for his wife and kids—we decided to help him out. He was helped by us all tutoring him; we also helped him out during testing—allowing him a peek or two at someone else's answer sheet.

He was helped on a very strategic, make-or-break test. After the test was graded, he was invited into an office, and we never saw him again! Finally, it became clear that, with everyone helping him, even the instructors looking the other way, this could go on no longer. We found out what actually happened. He not only copied the answers from a classmate—he copied **every** answer. But he also wrote his benefactor's name down on his answer booklet instead of his own. This is what tilted the scales. He had to go back to the surface Navy, where he could fit into a less-taxing job assignment, where more brawn than brains was required.

## Story: Topless Bar

How about this? Topless bars were a new trend around the country, but they were few and far between. Dam Neck, Virginia, was on the coast, but definitely in the boondocks. The nearest town of note was Virginia Beach, which was a sleepy beach resort town during our time. It is not that way today. So, on the outskirts of town, a new bar was being built, and it definitely advertised as the "Only topless bar within fifty miles." The word spread, and we were amped up waiting for the big opening day. We all tried to act cool—like it was not a big deal, BUT truth be told, every swinging dick (heterosexual) on the base was preparing for this major event. The night of nights

## My Early Days in the Navy

finally arrived, and the place was packed. Much to our surprise, the only ones topless in the joint were the male waiters! This was not what we were expecting. Controlled mayhem ensued, however, there was no fighting, no breaking of furniture or bottles, because it was well understood that none of us could afford any jail time—civilian or Navy.

After quite a bit of verbal offerings, we exited and never ever went near that dive again. And, in record time, the establishment went totally out of business because of their fucked-up idea of a joke.

### New Orders

Then came a big day back at school. We were going to get our orders to our first submarine assignment. It had been a hard and bumpy road to arrive at this point. Now everything we had worked toward had arrived. Final exams were over. I passed all of the written, oral, and hands-on practical portion of a detailed exam to prepare me for a prestigious assignment onboard a complex nuclear submarine of the United States Navy. Was I proud? You can bet your ass on that! I was part of something so few have the privilege of doing.

I was informed that I had been ordered to join the brand-new commissioning crew of the *USS Nathan Hale* SSBN 623 Boat, presently under construction at Electric Boat General Dynamics in Groton, Connecticut. I was thrilled and a little awestruck.

# C. Building Submarines

efore getting into my new life building submarines, I have to diverge again and tell you this little story.

## Story: Close Call

One of my classmates had introduced me to his sister via a phone call he made home during our stay at Dam Neck. She and I subsequently talked a number of times, keeping the conversation cordial. But my friend Jim Roberts had started calling me "brother-in-law."

Just before departing Dam Neck, there was talk of the possibility of getting per diem money to live off base and dine at places of our choice. Even though we were so close to Sub Base New London, they could not accommodate all of us. Consequently, per diem could be granted to us, and it was a tidy sum—in excess of $350 a month, which at that time was a lot of dough. However, there was some doubt as to whether this was actually going to happen.

Back to Jim Roberts and his sister, Adele. Jim wanted me to go to his home in Lee, Massachusetts, for two weeks of leave, which was granted to us after Dam Neck graduation. I decided that I did not want to get involved with a girlfriend-type of responsibility, so I told Jim that I was going straight to my sub to check in. He pissed and moaned quite a bit, but he finally accepted the fact that I would not be going with him. One of our mutual school friends invited himself to go with Jim in my place. And guess what? A year later, he and Adele were married! How about that? Take this news for what it is worth; now I will break protocol and tell you something shocking. They got divorced a couple of years later. She should have pursued her first love—ME! Oh, well, another example of an impatient woman.

—⚓—

Let's get back to the Navy scuttlebutt—the true form of communication within the Navy. Scuttlebutt is big-time gossip on steroids. If there is any doubt, you can be assured that once a rumor hits the scuttlebutt level, it is certain to be fact. This elevates it to the "This Ain't No Bullshit" status. People and ships will move.

I apologize—a point I failed to mention. Jim Roberts' orders were similar to mine. He was assigned to a new sub being built at General Dynamics in close proximity to my new sub. His new sub was the *USS Daniel Webster* SSBN 626. Now the

## My Early Days in the Navy

importance of all of these words is this. Jim had no girlfriend to go back to, and his leave time would be bullshitting with old high school chums and maybe having a drink or two with friends. Here is the relevance of this detail.

I checked into the sub's new construction office that was on the shipyard property on what they called a *living barge*. It looked like a ferryboat with all of the open spaces made into offices, with a functioning galley. It was a floating self-contained city with sleeping quarters one deck above. Because the galley and living spaces were not activated and not ready for occupancy, I was given a check for $375. Yes, another, per diem. But Jim did not get the same. I spoke with Jim on the phone, and I could tell he was not a happy camper. He had committed to a fishing trip that would take up his two-week leave, and he would lose all of that per diem. Poor decision on his part, if you ask me.

## 1. Electric Boat General Dynamics

Let me tell you about the shipyard at Electric Boat General Dynamics. It is a BIG OPERATION. Approaching the security office, one notices scores of time clocks with punch-in and punch-out stations. It seems like overkill, since there are so many. During my check-in process to get my credentials so that I could come and go from the shipyard, a siren went off, and out of nowhere thousands of workers rushed up a hill to get to the clocks to punch out for lunch. I stood back in amazement at this spectacle of thousands of *yard birds* (as they were affectionately called) and watched as this choreographed mass of humanity walked up the hill and efficiently passed through the time-clock stations. Many of them headed off to the nearby bars—yes, drinking establishments. This was surely a true-to-life experience.

After this avalanche of humanity subsided and my credentials were set and in hand, I was officially a junior yard bird, and the grand adventure was underway. My living arrangement was with one of the older sailors from my Dam Neck experience. His name was Danny Dole. He was one of the few in our class who was younger than the old salts but four or five years older than us young studs. Dan and his wife, Judy, rented me a room in their home and to my delight, threw in meals. Judy was a wonderful cook. It was a real win-win situation for me.

## Raw Steel Becomes a Submarine

My second day at the shipyard was a day of exploration and my first time walking into and onto my future home—a massive steel pipe assembled of many, many segments, eventually becoming a submarine. My first steps onboard were through a gaping square hole in the side of the future submarine, more specifically, at the lower level of the future missile compartment. I proceeded up and down all over this maze of scaffolding and ladders and temporary decking. I was totally confused, but filled with pride, to know that I was blessed to be a part of something so spectacular. Looking back on it, I knew that I felt like I was stepping on the Starship *Enterprise*. I loved every minute of every new exposure.

My Early Days in the Navy

## Story: A Sad One

There is a sad note from the end of my first day at the shipyard. I was now part of that mass of humanity to exit the shipyard at the end of the day. Remember the hill leading up to the punch-out clocks? All of a sudden, a major disturbance occurred at the middle of the hill. In the rush, someone fell, and the crowd stomped all over one of the workers before the onslaught could be slowed to a crawl and offer help to the poor soul. It was a warm day, and this fellow had a coat on—strange for those conditions. The guy was gasping for air. Good Samaritans struggled to get his coat off, and when they did, much to everyone's surprise…it was revealed that the full torso of his body was wrapped in heavy copper wire, which he was obviously trying to steal! He was rushing up the hill, and the exertion and warm temperature caused his body to demand more oxygen. Because the copper wire restricted and constricted his ability to drag in the necessary air and because of the time needed to unravel the wire, this stupid fuck died a horrible death—ironically by his own hand. Sadly, there would be other deaths in the shipyard during my stay there.

—⁂—

The day-to-day routine was full of challenges and adventures. We were a limited number of crewmembers, and it would take the entire crew many more months to put together the sub. We were representative of the United States Navy Ships Procurement. That meant we were not only crewmembers; we were inspectors ensuring that construction was done correctly and by the book. An example of our very necessary presence was never more evident than in the story I am about to reveal.

## Story: Precision Is Key

In the wee hours of the midnight shift, a crewmember noticed a mass of gray, gritty debris near where a welder was actually welding part of two hull segments. The hull was made of 2-and-½-inch-thick HY80 steel that had to be heated to 180 degrees to make the weld as perfect as possible. The gray grit caused this crewmember to investigate further, and what he uncovered was to shake up the entire shipyard and submarine construction schedule. All welding on three submarines came to a screaming halt. The gray, gritty substance was what is called *flux*. It is a coating on welding rods to aid the melting of the welding rod's adherence to the metal surface it was being applied to. It takes literally millions of welding rods to complete the hull of a submarine.

Now back to the discovery. The crewmember noticed over the shoulder of the welder that the welder was doing something so disastrously wrong that he rushed to the most senior Naval representative available and made his report. The weld process—burning or applying thousands of welding rods—is laborious and demands a lot of patience and concentration. However, the welder under question was doing something that could affect not only our submarine but every submarine this fucker ever worked on. He figured a way of burning all of the welding rods that were issued to him for the shift. All welding

## My Early Days in the Navy

rods had to be used or turned in. A very important accounting of rods had to be maintained for safety's sake. Instead of burning welding rods, which meant numerous coatings of long, molten ribbons of material, this sicko broke off the flux coatings on the rods and proceeded to fill the void with bare metal rods, and then he just welded over them to hide where melted rods should have been applied. Do you get the picture? He was cutting corners that would ultimately endanger the integrity of the hull of the submarine—with 140 men onboard with nuclear reactors, nuclear torpedoes, and nuclear missiles!!!

The shit hit the fan. This so-called welder was taken off in chains. The aftermath of the incident was that every weld of every sub at Electric Boat that this fool had ever worked on had to be magna-fluxed X-rayed. The ripple effect was going to be felt throughout the fleet, as numerous problems were discovered. That was the first of many bizarre and shocking events to follow. Shipyards are not for the faint of heart.

—⚒—

### *Story: On the Lighter Side*

In the missile compartment of the sub after the head was complete to a rough status, I noticed that all of the stainless steel was covered with cardboard to save and protect the stainless. Weeks went by, and I noticed the cardboard blocking off the entry to the commode had been altered. I poked around, and much to my surprise, I discovered the commode area had been converted into a bedroom of sorts. Picture the commode with enough rags and debris stuffed strategically to make the commode into a reclined bed. Now this is the best part.

A person was just sleeping away with an alarm clock prominently displayed on a shelf behind his head. Would you believe it? This ain't no bullshit. I had to shake him to wake him up. However, when he did wake, he started spouting off a lot of information that I was not asking for. He explained to me that he was a schoolteacher, and he worked the midnight shift here at Electric Boat. He told me that, after teaching school all day, he would go home to spend the evening with his family; then, when his wife went to sleep, he headed off for his second job at E.B. He had made an arrangement with his night-shift boss—so this was how he got some rest.

The fact is, that, eventually, it became obvious there were many workers who had these special arrangements. During the heyday of the accelerated submarine building boom, there were several ways to set up many under-the-table deals that financially benefitted foremen and workers.

This fellow went on to explain that his sleep time happened at E.B., and in the morning, since he never got dirty at work, he went right to his high school teaching job. He was able to do this because he gave up half of his paycheck to his boss/foreman. Like I said, because of the massive shipyard confusion and more bodies/workers than were really necessary, boondoggles flourished during times like this.

Because of all the noise from this guy, the immediate area filled with gawkers, and, eventually, my duty officer entered the picture and took over. After interviewing me and the "teach," I was no longer needed. I left the area, and E.B police

## My Early Days in the Navy

took over. The next day I checked out the impromptu bunk arrangement, and it had been sealed up so well it could never be utilized again. In the months to come, one more tucked-away impromptu bunk was found onboard our sub above the auxiliary tank #2. This was discovered because of an ongoing and recurring check for such cozy arrangements during the remainder of our time in the shipyard.

—⁂—

### *Story: Contractor Bids*

Here is a real sophisticated deal that rewrote the book of SCAMS. Contractors supplied many pieces and parts—all handled by bid—to build these submarines. It seems that a certain group of contractors were losing bid after bid, until one of them put in a bid, for a certain brass valve body, so far below true cost that a detailed investigation had to be conducted. After a year of intense undercover scrutinizing, it was discovered that the Electric Boat General Dynamic Foundry, located right onboard the shipyard property, had a side business making their own brass valve bodies, which they smuggled out of the shipyard to a warehouse in Mystic, Connecticut, repackaging the valve bodies and delivering them back to E.B. And, of course, it was at a tremendous profit.

Imagine employees of E.B. getting paid big bucks with plenty of overtime available. Add to that, using E.B. time and raw materials and manufacturing their own company's brass products. And here is the kicker. E.B. drivers, E.B. security guards, and a few other key people made all this happen efficiently, until their greed did them in. The human psyche is self-destructive…not knowing when to stop. This sort of chance-taking is like a living lie—the lie has to get bigger and bigger until the lie gets out of control, and loose ends become the pitfall. When one lives with truths, the facts never change, and there is never a doubt. When you live within a lie, you have to constantly try to remember the details of the lie. This becomes impossible, and a downfall is imminent.

## Shipyard Complexities

Do you get the gist of my life as a sailor? It was quite unusual. My sub-mates and I were not in the so-called regular Navy. We were not on a military base with all of its ceremonies and correctness. Nor were we on any organized efficient vessel with no yard birds around. We Navy types (amongst 5000 plus yard birds) had in our ranks some of the most brilliant and talented men and women in the world. And I was proud to be amongst them. I grew up and matured a great deal because of them. I loved all of my yard-bird friends.

### *Story: Living Arrangements*

Things were not looking so good on the home front. My living arrangements became tenuous. I would often help out around the house while I was living at Danny and Judy's home. Dan

## My Early Days in the Navy

was an outstanding submarine sailor, and he knew his shit extremely well, but when he got home, he couldn't leave the Navy behind, and his home life suffered because of his need for a regimented lifestyle every hour of the day. I knew that he and Judy were having some heated words, and I would make myself scarce on those occasions—not wanting to exacerbate the situation. Well, it wound up that Dan did not like the fact that I would help do dishes and sweep the floor after consuming a meal that I had shared with them. He was a staunch believer that that was Judy's job and her job only. So, my time with them soon came to an end after I had the audacity to repair a leg on their sofa. According to Dan, I was usurping his authority and position in his own home, and I had to make other living arrangements.

Funniest part of the whole deal was that, at work, we never spoke of the friction we experienced ever again. Dan was a Jekyll-and-Hyde kind of guy, but he was also a damned good sub sailor. Fact is, I was ready to leave Dan and Judy's and pile in with sub-mates in a living arrangement called *snake ranching*. It was a house with lots of bedrooms and at least two bathrooms where everyone lived by a strict code— "Whatever you hear or witness stays here!" And you cleaned up your own mess and didn't eat or drink anyone else's food or beverages. Parties were always on…sort of a requirement of living there. Someone was always going to work with a substantial headache.

One day I came back to the snake ranch after my shift at the shipyard and found one of my mates in the middle of an artistic adventure. Under the influence of much firewater, my old friend, Gary, had paints and easel assembled, and he was painting a naked lady in the living room. There on the couch was a very naked and good-looking lady. This was Gary's version of a "casting couch." By the way, she, too, was inebriated, and what Gary had on canvas looked more like what a child would produce in kindergarten art period than any kind of masterpiece. His shtick to pick up gals was to honor them through painting them nude. With enough booze applied, the young ladies didn't much give a damn about the final product.

## Story: My First Motorcycle

I had been having trouble getting around town, so I finally committed and settled on buying a motorcycle. Just outside of the Sub Base New London, a gentleman by the name of Steve Chan owned and operated a motorcycle shop. I visited him quite often because he let me help him on my time off. And watching this little old, crotchety character work always amazed me. To check the presence of current in the wiring on a motorcycle he had been working on, he would use his naked finger to do so. Many times, I heard him say, "Fuck, yes!" or go on bare-finger testing until he got zapped a good one.

Steve started carrying a new line of motorcycles called Honda. His mainstay or product line had always been Harleys, but he was willing to try this new line out, and he urged me to help him by giving me a good price, so as to get this cycle on the roads of New London to show it off. So, yes, I became one of the first in America to own a Honda—definitely the first in

## My Early Days in the Navy

Connecticut, since Steve was the only authorized dealership in all of New England.

I was the proud owner of a Honda Dream. I had never driven a motorcycle in my life. So, when all of the paperwork was done and the time came for me to ride off into the motorcycle sunset all by my lonesome, Steve and his lead mechanic gave me instructions, and, with one lesson, off I went. With old snow still on parts of Steve's parking lot, I drove out veering off-track and into the snowy zone. I plowed through (motorcycle staying upright), wheels parting the snow, and my feet acting like scoops digging into the snow, as snow was shooting up my shoe tops and then flying up under my pant legs. It was not a pretty sight—or an experience I would ever want to duplicate. I managed to get out of the snow and back on dry land. And then I had to shift the transmission with my left toe (my first time ever doing that) and enter the main road. Picture this! The clutch is in your left hand; you shift with your left toe; you brake with your right hand and right foot, always remembering to steer and, most importantly, watch out for the drivers who hate motorcycles and, more specifically, the rider!

Meanwhile the witnesses back at the parking lot of the dealership were cheering because I had made it into the flow of traffic without killing myself. I rode and practiced all of my new skills, and I was stoked—loving the wind on my face and the plastered bugs on my teeth. I became part of a select group of motorcyclists, and I enjoyed the raised-arm gesture motorcycle owners share when passing on the road. I think this is a nicety and tradition lost in the present-day motorcycle world. (My love for motorcycling continued to grow, and I eventually owned five different bikes.)

On that first day, though, when I got back to the dealership, an impromptu celebration began, and much beer was consumed, because I was actually not just a new purchasing customer, I was part of the little family at this dealership. I was one of the troops, and I was very proud of that status.

## Life on the Barge

Time marched on, and, eventually, the galley and living quarters were renovated and activated onboard the living barge. And, yes, per diem was cut off. A number of us moved onboard. The accommodations were not like the Ritz by any means. It was rather Spartan and absolutely without charm or coziness. My junior status made me eligible for what they called mess cooking in the Navy—K.P. (kitchen police) in the other services.

My roving the shipyard would be curtailed for a while, but when you are given a lemon, squeeze it, and make lemonade. And that's what I did daily. I had heard that the food in the submarine Navy was superb and that the food onboard the barge was fabulous. That became reality to me when I made friends with a Filipino cook by the name of Ernesto. He and the other cooks would fix meal after meal for the main chow line, but Ernesto would fix many of his native meals that he was raised on in the Philippines, on a separate stove. He always invited me to dine with him, and I joyfully did—with great

## My Early Days in the Navy

gusto. I was treated to chicken adobo, pork adobo, pancet, shrimp, fish, and lobster—all so delicious. I can still taste it now as I am writing these words, and my mouth is watering. You'll discover that, throughout my Navy career, I became very skilled at forming relationships with great cooks!

Meanwhile a big problem arose in the scullery, where all of the dishes and utensils were washed. A couple of the scullery crew started experiencing burning hands from a chemical reaction with the dish detergent. It seems that a tub that looked like the proper detergent was actually a container of tri-sodium sulfate, and, in concentrated applications, it would, of course, burn bare skin and, if allowed to soak, would eat the shiny metal finish off of all the flatware. And that is what happened to the flatware. All the utensils took on a look of gray slate. Basic first aid became necessary; new flatware was purchased, and all was back in a smooth operating mode.

To make mess cooking a little more enjoyable, we would do something called *plugging a watermelon*. Picture cutting a small circular hole in the melon, opening a bottle of rum, inverting the bottle, and then plugging it into the melon. The melon was then hid in the back of the large walk-in chill box, and, eventually, the melon absorbed every ounce of the rum. Quietly the word was passed to the friends of the mess cooks, and quite surreptitiously, the privileged friends of the mess cooks consumed the melon. And, of course, the mess cooks' daily grind was made more enjoyable with a little bit of this liquid lubrication, as we called it.

This period in my submarine life was a necessary evil, and every submariner has to go through it. Getting time off was a real pain in the ass, which was one day at a time, if it happened at all. Plus, since you lived onboard the barge, if they needed additional help in the galley, they would interrupt your downtime and put you back to work. Sucky pooh.

## Story: Righting a Wrong

Eventually, we, the mess cooks, became really efficient, and we convinced the cooks that we could earn a full weekend off by working really hard to cover all aspects of the galley. That worked! Half of the mess gang got a full weekend off, and we, the mess men who were left behind, handled everything totally fine with absolutely no problems. When the next weekend rolled around and my crew and I were to have a weekend off, the senior cook informed us at the last minute that we could not have our weekend off. I told him in no uncertain terms, "No fucking way" were we going to be screwed out of our turn for some well-needed time off. It didn't matter to me that this guy, the cook, was so senior to me that he could destroy me easily. I didn't care. He told me to shut my big effin' mouth or he would shut it for me. Now I got really bold and told him to call the head chief—Chief Winans, a character who was more like a used-car salesman, with a slick, shit-eating smile on his face.

Let me back up a minute. To supply our galley, we had to go to the main base to resupply our needs. On each trip, a different select mess cook would be the muscle to lead and unload the truck or trucks. Chief Winans would always drive a pickup truck, and at least one mess cook would accompany

## My Early Days in the Navy

him. This proved to be his downfall. On at least two trips, I was his so-called muscle. The stupid bag-of-shit would put select food items from meat to potatoes in fairly large quantities in his truck and then drive to his house and have me unload this truck into his home for illegal personal use. Because of the quantity, he had other friends come by later that day. They were other cooks and crooks, if you haven't figured that out already.

I stood my ground, and another cook stepped in, thinking my request was very fair, which was to call Winans at his home. This cook was an old submarine cook with a lot of no-bullshit experience. He did not like Winans because of his slick style of so-called leadership and the fact that Winans was a recent surface-craft puke trying to switch to the submarine Navy.

The call was made, and Chief Winans, who was the one who pulled our weekend in the first place, wanted to talk with me. He was screaming mad at me and threatened to destroy me and said how dare I demand to talk to him at all. My chance to talk finally came. It was a make-or-break moment for me. I would either make my case, or I would be leaving the Navy, if I misjudged my position. I told Winans that if he fucked with our weekend off, I would go to our commanding officer and tell him of the trips to his home and the offloading of thousands of dollars' worth of food, and that there were five or six of us strong who could end his career. He called me a no-good motherfucker and told me to give the phone to the duty cook. I left the room, and I was scared shitless wondering why in the hell I'd done this. I felt like a fool fighting a battle that could ruin me—whether I was right or wrong.

When the duty cook came to find me, he said to me, "What do you think happened?" Well, the cook told me to enjoy my weekend, and that was that. The other cook slapped me on my back and said, "I love it! I hate that son-of-a-bitch."

So, what would it be like when I returned to the living barge on Monday to hear some outstanding news? Shock upon shock: I was not needed as a mess cook any more, and so far, I was pleased with what I had accomplished. There were no more ramifications. But an update to the story is that the crook (Winans) was caught selling Navy/government provisions out of his home—through no help of mine. He was court-martialed out of the Navy—a sixteen-year career washed down the drain. Can you imagine what he had been getting away with for those sixteen years before finally being caught? I had absolutely NO sympathy for his prosecution. And for weeks and months to come, additional stories of his crooked shenanigans were exposed.

Well, upward and onward! My life as a mess cook was over and done with. But the memories live on.

## 2. Submarine Launch

Now it was balls-to-the-wall—total commitment onboard the sub. We were getting the best submarine built, with safety and watertight integrity being our utmost goal to create this watchdog for the U.S. Navy. In the Submarine Navy, we were a unique and—I don't mind saying—a special community of

## My Early Days in the Navy

adventure-minded, thrill-seeking, very professional men—the best America had to offer!

Submariners have to know not only their specific trained specialty—they must have a working knowledge of everyone else's specialty onboard the sub. That means that each and every man has to know every valve, every switch, and every piece of machinery onboard the submarine. The ever-present theory is that, in any sudden emergency, any given crewmember might be the only one who could take action in order to save the sub and everyone onboard. So, for months on end, we crawled around the sub learning about *all* of its idiosyncrasies and intricacies.

While in this pursuit of knowledge, there were many opportunities to have some fun. For example, when a friend of mine was sent to get 20 feet of *water line*. (I hope that you caught that.) Or on another day, one might be sent to get a *bucket of steam*. A lot of good belly laughs resulted when the individual in pursuit of these fairytale requests traveled all over the shipyard to fulfill them. They were directed to piers, docks, offices, as well as the monstrous production building (some as large as a modern enclosed sports arena) trying to satisfy those impossible tasks. All the while, at every shipyard in which the U.S. Navy has ever been located, this game has existed. Most yard birds go along with the program and give them ever-more-bogus directions to seek their treasure.

In the end, qualifying in submarines was a hard, very difficult, and time-consuming endeavor—made a little lighter with many moments of levity and great fun. Qualifying was so difficult because we were working with a brand-new submarine that had zero operating time, and half of the equipment was not even installed yet. With our books, called *Piping Tabs* (filled with blueprints of piping and electrical layouts) and our notepads, we trudged on.

## The Launching

The day finally came when all the gaping holes in the submarine were welded up and all the electronic consoles were installed, signifying that a special day would soon be upon us, that is, *The Launching*. Relatively few crewmembers had been assembled at that point, so that meant we would need to be topside in uniform on the day and ride the submarine down the *Ways*.

All submarines and ships, since ancient times, started high and dry on land for obvious reasons, whether they were made of wood or metal. When the watertight integrity was secure, the launching date was scheduled. For the crew, that meant finding our dress uniforms, and that became a problem because all of us had lived off base for so long that our uniforms had become scattered. Even though we had moved aboard the living barge, the accommodations were definitely not like a cruise ship. Add to that, for me, ever since the first day I checked in onboard the submarine, I had worn nothing but my Navy jeans, hardhat, and safety shoes. In reality we looked more like yard birds, except that our hard hats were white with a United States Naval insignia on it. What I am trying to say in far too many words is that we looked more like *McHale's Navy*—far less official than the submarine occupants on the main base a couple of miles away.

# My Early Days in the Navy

The submarine launch date was set—23 November 1963. Sound a little familiar? Yes, it was the day after President Kennedy's assassination. The day arrived. With the uniform issues well behind us, and dignitaries from around our nation assembled, a somber launch was going to take place, even though there had been a national tragedy the day before. As we listened to all of the wonderful but joyless words carried over the loudspeaker system, we, the assembled crewmembers and a number of yard birds, went for a monumental ride on our brand-new submarine—riding it the entire length (425') and breadth (33') down the Ways as it entered the water for the first time. The *USS Nathan Hale* SSBN 623 Boat took a major step toward its intended purpose.

The ride down the Ways was mind-boggling, to say the least. This monstrous hunk of HY80 steel slid down well-greased wooden slips, and in an instant this submarine was floating for the first time—with sirens blaring and tugboats throwing water-cannon geysers into the air. We still had a long way to go, but we had a watertight hull with no leaks.

Before the crew of the *USS Nathan Hale* left the shipyard, we experienced two additional launches—the *USS Flasher* SS 613 and the *USS Daniel Webster* SSBN 626 Boat. Both of these boats were launched the same day, which was a pretty spectacular event in itself. Some of us had to ride the *Flasher* down to Ways because they did not have many crewmembers at the shipyard at the time. Imagine the odds of physically being part of two submarine launches and witnessing three in total in my then-short Naval career.

After all of the glitz of the launch and the ceremonies came to an end, the heads of many civilians were filled with amazement. They were awestruck observing the launch experience and were made aware of what had been going on at Electric Boat General Dynamics. So much so that at shift's end, the bars outside of E.B. became swamped with an unbelievable number of men as they swarmed in to quench their thirst and celebrate. And this was a scene that I feel compelled to describe to you.

## *Story: Side Bar*

Prior to a shift's end, the barmaids started a ritual of filling more than one hundred glasses of beer, which literally covered the bar surface from one end to the other. Behind the bar at Elfie's, there was an oversized snifter glass—so big a toddler could sit in it. At shift's end, the workers streamed in, dug into their pockets, pulled out their quarters and half-dollar coins, tossed them into the snifter, picked up the appropriate number of pre-filled glasses of beer, and then stepped aside to allow the next guys to gain access to the bar. The barmaids were eagle-eyed. They could spot a sleight-of-hand transaction immediately and quickly get restitution. This shift-changing ritual occurred three times a day, seven days a week. The first time I witnessed this phenomenon, my heart rate increased, and I was thrust into an event that is etched into my memory bank. It could never be duplicated, and I will call it "controlled mayhem personified."

# My Early Days in the Navy

―᭝―

## Story: Navy Cooks

When I got back to the sub that night, I was told there was a problem onboard the living barge. We had, by then, been eating onboard the barge, enjoying a tasty item that was served at lunch—a particular onboard cook's specialty—spicy chili. This cook sometimes got a little carried away with the quantity of hot spices he packed into the recipe. A pre-meal taste test by the head cook determined that the item should be pulled off of the steam line (serving line), because it was far too hot. Instead of it being dumped, it was later discovered that that pot found its way into the big walk-in chill box.

Some hearty souls decided to heat it up even more and serve it as a mid-ration, affectionately called "mid-rats" or "the midnight meal" for the off-going and the on-coming Naval personnel. These sailors, being up for a challenge, readily realized that this chili was unusually hot, but they had to prove that they were up to the challenge, and they ate this *lava in a bowl*. When I came onto the scene, the first ambulance was there, and medical personnel were attempting to pump stomachs on about four different submariners in quick order. These poor bastards were writhing with stomach cramps and puking what they could on their own.

All of the mayhem at Elfie's Bar and the mayhem at the barge made for a night that I will never forget. Everybody lived—after much discomfort. And the cook, James Derricott, was ordered to stick to Naval recipe cards from that point on, or he would be court-martialed and given a dishonorable discharge! I might add that Naval recipe cards were not to be fucked with. Imagine a cook improvising a recipe to his own personal satisfaction before a big Naval engagement, and the type of mayhem I just described ensued. That could result in a number of crewmembers not being able to man their battle stations. All hell could break loose. Not a good thing.

This so-called cook's name was Derricott, and I am not protecting this fool's identity, although he was let off lightly because of a technicality. Fact was, he had a personality like a *bent shit can* and should have been thrown out of the Navy a long time before this incident. This guy had the ability to take the best recipes the Navy had, follow it step-by-step without deviation, and the end-product would taste like shit. Happy to say that he was assigned to the other crew. Thank God!

## The Blue Crew and the Gold Crew

All Fleet Ballistic Missile Submarines had two crews—a Blue Crew and a Gold Crew. This enabled the submarines (ballistic missile types) to stay at sea year-round. That meant I, along with our other Gold Crew members, would only be in this shithead's company for five days four times a year during change of commands. The cooks we wound up with after the crews were finalized happened to be the best of the best. One of them happened to be a Filipino by the name of Ernesto Diaz, whom I have already mentioned. Everything Ernesto touched was far and above better than it could possibly be because he loved what he did. He was a true chef with the moniker of

# My Early Days in the Navy

*Navy Cook.* So once again, I had a relationship with a fantastic Filipino cook who invited me to join him to savor the separate meal he cooked in addition to what he had to cook per Naval orders for the crew. And because of our friendship, he always included me to eat with him and experience his golden touch—dishes like chicken adobo, pork adobo, Filipino shish kebab, lumpia, and, my favorite, pancet. This dish falls into the category of poor man's food—pork or chicken bits, rice noodles, garlic, spring onion, and a little peanut oil. My mouth is watering trying to write this.

All right, what the hell am I trying to say here? Fact is, if you have not heard it before, submariners are the best-fed members of any military service! Only the best cooks were allowed onboard submarines. The gentleman, Mr. Derricott of chili fame, pulled another stunt long after the one I described, and he was sent to the surface Navy and eventually was persuaded to change rates (job description) and became a boatswain's mate—never to cook again.

## *Story: Missile Compartment*

In the missile compartment, the shipyard personnel laid our new vinyl flooring on all three levels, and the yard guys only put heavy brown paper down to protect it. I put out the word that we had to find some canvas somewhere in the shipyard. One of my friends and I took it up as a challenge—whoever got a bona fide roll of canvas for the job would win a sumptuous meal at a well-loved restaurant in town. Off we went, and, after I'd searched high and low, I discovered a brand-new roll of the perfect canvas—manna from heaven. It seemed to have my name written all over it, and I could taste the veal parmesan at Anthony's Italian Bistro.

It was going to be a challenge with no transportation available. Nobody seemed to notice me, so I picked up an unusually heavy parcel and with a thief's guilty grin on my face, I strode off in the direction of my submarine. The task was harder than I realized, but I was going to win the bet and be a hero in the eyes of my superiors by protecting our new vinyl in the missile compartment. At times I thought I would die from the weight of the roll of canvas; my muscles ached, and I was sweating profusely. However, I got the parcel to the sub, and, coincidentally, my friend was at the brow (gangway), coming off the sub. Suddenly, I felt a tap on my shoulder, and I put my load down, wondering what this yard bird was wanting to talk with me about.

I learned that rolls of canvas from a distant location in the shipyard were requisitioned for my submarine to specifically cover the temporary paper placed over our new vinyl. The yard bird told me that he was waiting for shipyard transportation to do what I managed to foolishly break my ass doing! He spotted me, and he decided to go ahead and bust my ass even further, entertaining himself with each and every step. The best part of this was that I was delivering the goods to the proper location, which made his job even easier. So, my friend, Bill, laughed at my expense, and, even though I'd produced a roll of canvas, it did not add up to winning the bet. Consequently—NO parmesan!

The shipyard guy ultimately became a friend of mine, and we shared a beer or two every so often; the more tipsy we

## My Early Days in the Navy

got, the better the canvas story became! He shared that story with anybody who would listen.

—⚓—

## Story: Tragic Accidents Happen

One day there was a terrible accident above the Auxiliary Machinery Space #2 on the main deck. A buoy in a cradle compartment had two doors which opened in the middle like a clamshell. The doors' back edges disappeared into a free flood area of the super structure, practically touching the pressure hull—essentially two doors turned their back edges into guillotines. The doors were being tested for opening and closing purposes. For safety's sake, the testing yard person was stationed purposely with headphones and a mouthpiece to constantly be in contact with the yard personnel below decks operating the hydraulics to open and close the buoy compartment doors.

Before testing commenced, the topside guy took off his communication gear and entered the free flood area of the superstructure by one hatch in front of the buoy. He crawled through past the buoy apparatus and satisfied himself that all was clear and then exited the free flood area by another hatch on the aft side of the buoy. He then put his communication gear on and reported to his testing crew that he had crawled through the buoy superstructure area and that it was all clear. A moment later, the doors opened, and a blood-curdling scream was heard. An immediate reversal of the buoy door opening command was given, but it was too late. When the shipyard safety rep topside (guy #1) took off his headphones and mouthpiece to check the superstructure, at some point while he was crawling through, another yard guy (#2) entered the superstructure through the same hatch, unbeknownst to yard guy #1. By coming out at a different entry point, a perfect storm was created—#1 guy never saw #2 guy and vice versa. When the hatch opened, #2 guy was killed instantly. Needless to say, all testing procedures were re-written, and more testing personnel were stationed to prevent any reoccurrence.

Sorry to have added this terrible story to the book, but this life and the reality of heart-wrenching disaster are part of every day in the real world, and my submarine days in the Navy were certainly no exception.

## Story: Helping a Friend

One night I got a phone call onboard the work barge from a friend in trouble. He was caught driving with seven open beer cans in the car. Once upon a time, this was not considered a DUI offense. The open container was the only charge pending. However, he had a history of various moving violations that were piling up, and he was in a state of total frustration. He asked if I could come and bail him out. I said that I would. I got a ride to the New London police department. The bail was only $50—back in the day, folks, things were a little more reasonable. As we exited the police station, my friend told me

## My Early Days in the Navy

that he was going to sign his car over to me—Alan S. Votta—to reimburse me for bailing him out. He wanted no part of automobile ownership any longer! However, I thought he would change his mind when he sobered up. But he stuck to it, even though I told him I did not want the responsibility of a car myself and that I would sell it. He didn't care. So, a month later, I sold his old Buick for $500, and everybody was happy!

---

### Story: Dealing with the Law

Here's one story about dealing with the law that all worked out just fine. I was pulled over by the Groton, Connecticut Police Department. The officer felt that he had a sure violation on still another service member. Many servicemen have a license issued by their home state that does not need to be renewed during military service. But after leaving the service, it must be updated. The problem at hand, however, was that many of us active-duty members held home state licenses and also bought a car that was registered in another state. Plus, during the time of service, we all were transferred to another state several times. This predicament resulted in many service types in violation of the Tri-State Law—that is, license from one state, car registered in another state, and driving in still another state.

When I was pulled over (in violation of the above-mentioned Tri-State Law) I had to follow an idiot cop, who was treating me like a bank robber, back to his station. The station house was old and multi-purposed, and I felt like I was about to be submitted to a little bit of the northern version of *Deliverance*. I felt like I was about to be screwed royally. I had to sit among a handful of strangers (including the town drunk) who were about to receive justice, like me. The so-called judge was streaking through his court session, and it became apparent that I was being purposely overlooked, until I realized I was obviously going to be his last case of the day.

Finally, the courtroom emptied out, and only the judge, the officer who wrote the ticket, and I remained. The suspense was killing me, and the judge looked at me and said, "VOTTA! What the fuck are you doing in my court?" I almost fell down, and my head was in a spin. What the hell was going on? The judge then said to the ticketing officer, "I've got it from here." And the officer exited the courtroom.

I was completely puzzled. The judge then told me to follow him into his chambers. "Now what?" I said to myself. We entered his office, and he said, "Let's have some coffee and catch up." I was more stunned than before. The judge looked at me and said, "You don't remember me, do you?" I wracked my brain. Finally, he said, "Chinese 100." And then it all made sense. This guy was the chief instructor of the Submarine School when I had written the "Chinese 100" exam, and he was the one who'd sanctioned my unusual challenge. He looked so totally different as a civilian and out of uniform.

After much coffee was consumed and many stories swapped, my ticket was shredded, and an open invitation to visit him at the courthouse and/or his home was extended. His final remark to me on that day was that the Chinese 100

## My Early Days in the Navy

was one of his best humorous memories of his entire military career!

By the way, eventually the Tri-State Law was deemed prejudicial and scrapped nationwide.

---

## Story: Another—On the Lighter Side

A fellow crewmember who also happened to have been born and raised in New London, Connecticut, got in touch with me, asking me to help him and his dad take an automatic washing machine back to Sears. I had the time, and I wanted to get away from the shipyard and the dirt and the dust, so I volunteered. My friend Larry Brown came by and picked me up, and off we went to his parents' house in Mystic, Connecticut. I asked Larry about the washing-machine problem, and all Larry could say was, "Wait and see."

At Larry's parents' house, we quickly loaded the machine into his dad's pickup truck. With few words spoken, we were off to Sears Roebuck in downtown New London on State Street. Larry's dad parked conveniently in front of the main entrance, and he told Larry and me to wait there. Larry's dad went into Sears, and, after a very long time, he reappeared with an appliance salesman in tow. Larry and I got out of the truck, and his dad instructed us to climb up on the truck and toss (yes, toss!) that machine onto the sidewalk.

Larry was not surprised by this, but I surely was. Somewhat reluctantly I climbed up on the truck with Larry, and he indicated that, on the count of three, we should pick up the washing machine and toss it as instructed. Larry started counting, "One, two…" and all the while the salesman was beside himself shouting, "Stop! Stop! Stop!" Larry finally got to the number "three," and the machine bounced off the sidewalk; a few pieces scattered all over the place. The salesman was indeed rattled. Mr. Brown looked at him and said, "I told you the machine was a faulty lemon, and you refused to solve the problem for months. Now I am telling you flat out that you fucked with the wrong guy!" We drove away to the Western Electric Store, and Mr. Brown bought a new washing machine, which he took home and installed that very day.

The rest of the day included lots of belly laughs about what had transpired earlier in the day. I can still see the salesman's astonished look on his face watching the washing machine flying through the air and crashing to the ground.

## Story: Another Character

Before that day was over, I met up with another friend and fellow crewmember by the name of Jim Caudill, a real country boy from Elkton, North Carolina, which is in the middle of Surry County, best known for the movie *Thunder Road* about moonshiners and the special cars they souped up to outrun the *revenuers*, the cops. My friends, this is exactly how NASCAR was created. When the fast and souped-up moonshine delivery cars were not delivering white lightning,

## My Early Days in the Navy

the drivers would challenge one another on impromptu dirt tracks. The rest is history.

Back to Jim and me. Being with Jim was a delight and always entertaining because of his Andy Griffith personality. Jim and I met when he was assigned to the *Nathan Hale*. We hit it off right away. Jim was not just a young stud like me, he was an old salt, having already served onboard another submarine—an old WWII-type diesel submarine.

The first time we went out to hit a bar or two, Jim, the old salt, was surprised when he was asked for proof of age at the first bar we hit, but I wasn't. That shocked Jim. I soon realized that Jim could spend money—easily. If Jim had twenty bucks on him and he saw something for twenty bucks, whether he needed it or not, he would act on impulse and buy it in a heartbeat. This characteristic was to be Jim's—almost—downfall. Jim managed to buy himself a kinkajou. Yes, a kinkajou—a member of the racoon and bear family. I asked him, "Why? What the hell are you going to do with it?" His answer was, with a smile on his face, simply, "I had the money!"

After a couple of days trying to keep Kinky, Jim shipped the bear home. This is all so true. His dad received it, and, instead of placing the animal in a cage, they decided to incarcerate Kinky in the attic. Kinkajous are nocturnal, and it kept Jim's mom and dad up all night. But then Kinky escaped. Jim's dad called the local police, and they notified the local radio station. But here is the kicker: the police and radio station put out the description, "A kinkajou, a member of the bear family, has escaped, and please notify the police if you see it." Of course, the public heard only BEAR, and all of Elkton, North

Carolina, panicked. All work stopped, and people barricaded themselves in their houses. State Wildlife came in, and, in quick order, they found Kinky in a garbage can near Jim's mom's and dad's house. All calmed down again in Mayberry, RFD, better known as Elkton.

---

## 3. Around the Shipyard

### Story: Motorcycle Trips

Remember Jim Roberts? He tried to get me to marry his sister Adele. Well, Jim was then aboard his sub, the *USS Daniel Webster* SSBN 626, which was under construction in the shipyard. We were so busy aboard our respective subs that socializing was quite restricted. However, Jim purchased a new motorcycle—a Matchless, a British bike. At that time, I traded my Honda Dream in for another British bike called a Norton Atlas, which was an absolute knockout at 750 ccs. When Jim and I could get some time off together, we rode off into the sunset with no great plan or destination in mind—the true biker experience—riding with a friend in a staggered formation, one slightly ahead of the other. (Cyclists never ride side-by-side. It's a big no-no for safety's sake.)

The rides through the country roads of New England were spectacular and invigorating. We would ride and stop to eat in unique restaurants and wonderful locations, and cap

## My Early Days in the Navy

off the day by staying overnight in an old-fashioned inn or B and B. Because Jim and I were associated with submarines and the Navy, we sort of became celebrities of the hour and were treated fantastically—sometimes with a free round of drinks. The wind in your face and gliding over the roadways seemed like a dream to me, and it was a natural high. Still to this day, everything about motorcycles, and, more specifically, *the ride*, rank in the top-five experiences of my life. As I write this, I find myself daydreaming and recounting some of the people I met and the scenes I was blessed to see along the way.

### Back at the Shipyard

Okay, back to the grind at the shipyard and the task at hand of building a nuclear submarine. My first day back, I was tasked with inspecting and signing off on a total sandblasting and reapplication of a special paint job inside a tank that all four torpedo tubes pass through. The previous paint job was chipping, which caused the gaskets to the giant valves to allow a huge flush of water to eject the torpedoes. The location was difficult to gain access to. It was actually a manhole in the superstructure of the sub, forward of the torpedo-room hatch. When you enter these tight quarters, you then have to wriggle your way through the anchor windlass frames and pipes. The tank appears, and the step-by-step checkout procedure to sign off on the job is completed.

Inspection complete and a job well done by the shipyard. We removed all shipyard gear and took down the temporary lighting; then we all exited the tank. We took a break, had a smoke or two, and then finally closed up the tank by putting a gasket and then the heavy access cover in place. It was like a manhole cover—slightly smaller and oval instead of round. We finished our exiting procedure, weaving our way through all of the obstacles, and finally put the superstructure cover on. Our complicated task was finished.

After I returned below decks and resumed my duties, I turned in my paperwork on the inspection I had just completed. Not long after, a high-ranking Naval Engineer Inspector came to me and informed me that the task I'd just completed had to be done by him. Therefore, we needed to assemble the entire tank repair and inspection team, open up the superstructure, string lights, and take the cover off of the tank all over again! After a bit of frustration, and as we uncovered the tank cover—to everyone's total surprise—a light was dancing around in the interior. We all froze and instantly realized that when we all previously exited and took the smoke break: a very quiet and unassuming shipyard *cleaner* had entered the tank without us realizing it. You need to pause and think about that for a minute! If this high-ranking Naval Engineer had decided that my inspection sufficed and he was too lazy to do the re-inspection, that shipyard cleaner would never have been missed, and he would have been terrorized when he was ready to exit the tank. NO ONE would have heard his screams! (Your imagination should be going wild at this point.)

The cleaner was still diligently doing his thing, but he started realizing that there was something strange going on. We never exchanged any words with him, and he abruptly exited the tank and the area. After a very long pause was observed

## My Early Days in the Navy

by us, I thanked God that we'd followed official protocol and the directions that saved this man's life. And, after that, the tank inspection procedures were rewritten to add an additional obligatory inspection.

I never saw that shipyard cleaner again, but a full investigation did occur. I was exonerated and cleared of any negligence. Instead, I was applauded and praised because I stayed with the inspection team, even though I did not have to, because the Naval Engineer was the one responsible. My presence expedited finding the shipyard cleaner sooner. If I had not helped, the re-inspection would have been held off until the next day, when they could assemble enough personnel to commence the whole procedure. Would there have been enough oxygen in the tank for the shipyard cleaner? That tank is watertight and below the waterline when the sub was out of dry dock.

After this incident, my attention to detail doubled—if not tripled. I had always been a stickler for detail, but I became obnoxious! I would never be put into a life-threatening situation ever again because of not thinking about possible ramifications of allowing myself to do an incomplete job.

### Testing the Sub

The day was coming ever so near to when this wondrous monster of HY80 steel and all manner of electronic, electric, hydraulic and pneumatic miracles of man's ingenuity would be taken to sea by my fellow crewmembers and me, and actually, purposely submerge this perfectly good submarine.

I am now realizing that had I kept a daily diary of just my exploits and experiences, and then decided to write a book, the outcome would and could become a multi-volume endeavor exceeding all of the *Star Trek* sequels. This book will be, I hope, a brief, but loving synopsis of a whole lot of wonderful experiences that are mine.

## Unveiling a Submarine

The day was upon us. After what seemed like a lifetime, the interior of the submarine was being unveiled. Tons of protective covering were being taken off of the equipment and surfaces inside the submarine. After all of that protective brown paper, canvas, and thick vinyl sheathing was removed, we almost looked like an operational submarine. We were still receiving new personnel on a daily basis to complete our full crew roster, as a very important time had arrived. We had to split all of the ship's personnel into two separate crews—the Blue Crew and the Gold Crew. This kind of took on the atmosphere of the NFL Draft!

By now, we knew most of the crewmembers, and we had an idea of who we might want on our crew. I went to the Gold Crew, and, through a lot of finagling, which was essentially negotiating to get who we felt was the cream of the crop on our team, we managed, I believe, to put together the best available of the two crews. For example, my weapons officer once got a citation for flying his personal airplane too low. He was obviously following the path of a highway—a big no-no in the pilot manual. He did this because he was terrible at

## My Early Days in the Navy

navigation! Our corpsman, our *doc,* when returning to the submarine base, almost wiped out the Marines protecting the gate, because he was totally snockered. He told the Marines his car was possessed and, therefore, he was not to blame. I might add that back in the day drinking was not discussed as a negative issue. There were three or four clubs on base throughout every military establishment with plenty of alcohol readily available. The real point here is that every crewmember was a very unique character unto himself, but when it came down to being professional, these characters congealed into a fighting force to be reckoned with.

## Admiral Rickover

This pile of steel, consisting of real *Star Trek* gadgets, was actually being prepped to go to sea and dive for the first time. That meant Admiral Hyman G. Rickover was going to be onboard the submarine—as was his custom—for the first dive of every new submarine built. Talk about people on their best behavior! Automatically, a number of very special steps were to be undertaken.

The first step was to locate and buy plenty of a certain brand of *lemon drops.* In addition to that, all chiefs onboard needed to have an extra uniform available, and all officers needed to be ready to stand guard duty outside of the stateroom the Admiral would occupy. And the periscope stand must be in pristine condition because that is where the Admiral usually spent most of his time onboard. The lemon drops were based on a fond memory Admiral Rickover had from his early days on diesel electric submarines. Lemon drops were one of the few luxuries onboard then, and they represented a special memory and good luck for him.

As was his custom, when the Admiral arrived (with little or no entourage), he was dressed in civilian clothes; and he invariably found a Chief Petty Officer onboard who was near his size, and he borrowed his uniform. He always forgot to give it back!

The officer standing guard was more special than one would suspect. Although it was not publicized, the Admiral interviewed every officer before being chosen by him to join his elite nuclear sub program. Admiral Rickover had a photographic memory, and he knew every officer better than the officer knew himself. Therefore, his guard duty would become his link to the sub, and he could get a feel for the personality of the sub crew and then talk nuclear stuff.

History will one day recognize Admiral Rickover as one of the most innovative and brilliant minds of the 20th century. And, in my opinion, had the U.S. government utilized his recommendations, the civilian nuclear power plant horrendous failures, like Three Mile Island and fifty-six other incidents, might not have happened, or they could have been reduced to possibly zero. Since Rickover was such a stickler for detail, quality control, and procedure, those failures might never have occurred.

My Early Days in the Navy

## Final Steps Before Sea Trials

Every day I became more impressed with what we had created and given birth to. The last step was a final complete exterior uniform paint job, and the hull number was applied on the sail for the first time—a big 623. Yes, the SSBN 623, the very next nuclear submarine, was about to be unveiled, commissioned, and added to the *Arsenal of Democracy*. Following that, our extensive sea trials would get underway.

The commissioning was held amidst a rather subdued and low-key atmosphere even though it was months after the assassination of President Kennedy. Due to the somber mood of the country, the joy was taken out of this normally festive day. The Navy band and all conversation was muted. However, we had a submarine to get ready for the United States Navy. The Show Must Go On!

## Part Two

## First Days at Sea

# A. Sea Trials

Sea trials are rigorous and exhausting, and the testing is endless—rightfully so. When our dive was successfully completed and we proceeded to our test depth, I felt so small with my flashlight in hand checking for leaks. The submarine let out some squeaks and pops, but no leaks of any sort. All of this took place with Admiral Rickover in the control room, up on the periscope stand, along with our captain and many Electric Boat engineers and techs as well as crewmembers.

One of the Electric Boat techs announced that a water leak was quite close to where the Admiral was sitting. The leak was from the previous location of the Type 11 periscope that had been installed but then completely dismantled, removed, and done away with. The scope was a high-tech sextant that now was being outmoded because of the introduction of the forerunner of the present-day GPS systems.

At day's end, we had a list of minor problems that were not earth-shattering but had to be reckoned with. After returning to the shipyard, it was discovered that the leak in the Type 11 periscope area was quite distressing. It seemed that some of the hull penetrations associated with the scope were never properly sealed up as per engineering design. We discovered the hull penetrations had temporary wooden plugs called DC plugs—quite insufficient in this sophisticated HY80 steel hull. Somehow they miraculously functioned well all during our sea trials and our deep dive! Get the picture? A couple of archaic devices made of wood might possibly have been instrumental in saving (or not saving) many lives in this brand-new submarine.

A proper investigation was undertaken, the holes were filled with proper HY80 steel plugs, and a couple of Navy careers were altered and destroyed. Electric Boat personnel were also dealt with in the most stringent way—fired and charged with neglect and industrial malfeasance. Their neglect might have created undue harm and the potential death of innocent people. This story, or this incident, is worthy of a book unto itself.

We had to march on and complete innumerable and fatiguing sea trials to show the world that we had produced another peace-keeping wonder with our sole purpose being deterrence—that is, to make our enemies realize they had overstepped boundaries and that we could react and make them pay a heavy price.

After sea trials and many tweaks and adjustments and crew training, our CO (Commanding Officer) received official orders to proceed to Charleston, South Carolina, to the United

First Days at Sea

States Naval Weapons Station and receive our first Polaris missiles and other arms and devices. We were then to proceed to Cape Canaveral (soon to be renamed Cape Kennedy for obvious and unfortunate reasons.) The startling realization that this shipyard experiment was now being transformed into a Fleet Ballistic Missile Nuclear Submarine with real arms and devices onboard was rather daunting and sobering.

## Story: A Little R&R

The missiles onboard would not have nuclear warheads, but they would be, instead, packed with electronic monitoring devices, because after Charleston, South Carolina, our destination was Cape Canaveral, to test our Polaris Missile Launch capabilities and Torpedo Tube Ejection Systems. At the Cape, many long, tiring hours ensued. Following that, we had a bus at our disposal for a little wind-down time that took the crew members into the downtown Cocoa Beach area for a little "R & R" at the local bars, restaurants, and clubs. On the first night, the bus managed to wipe out an awning at the Cocoa Beach Racquet Club! Perhaps the sobriety (or lack thereof) of the volunteer driver had something to do with it? I leave that question open.

For the poor souls who were not part of the fun of tearing down an awning, they were relegated to the Cinder Block Drink Spa near the docks of Port Canaveral. This was a charming submariners drinking spot devoid of personality or charm. It was really like the armpit of an experience but a place we loved because all of its previous guests, i.e., submariners who had visited this armpit prior to us, had added some decoration to note their love of this hole-in-the-wall joint. Plaques, flags, and memorabilia that only submariners could relate to lined the walls, which created a sense of submariner brotherhood.

One night after overindulging, we discovered a shovel and a cinder block nearby. With that equipment available, we carved into the turf a very convincing outline of a fresh grave. On the cinder block we wrote an epitaph to our favorite brand-new First Lieutenant J. P. Riley. This gentleman was a true legend in his own time. He was one of the characters back in the days of Dam Neck, Virginia, at Guided Missile School, who tied their warm beer cans to the bumper of a car and ran around base cooling the beer off. Update! Update! We discovered that if you put the beer into a metal trash can and shoot it with a $CO_2$ fire extinguisher, it cooled more quickly, and the beer was colder!

Back to the point. The grave looked so real with the headstone and a proper name applied in black magic marker that the Cape Canaveral Property Security Guards were convinced they had to dig into the persuasive-looking grave and investigate to guarantee that something sinister hadn't happened. Fact is that, instead of a major incident, a good laugh was had by all. That was then. Different day, and a whole different attitude were prevalent then. If this happened today, there would be fifty satellite trucks and a thousand reporters blithering and blathering about a major non-incident at Cape Canaveral.

First Days at Sea

# 1. *USS Thresher*

I have to pause and radically switch gears. Since we were actually still on Sea Trials, I have to reflect back to a day in the Electric Boat General Dynamic Shipyard when one could literally hear a pin drop. In this monolithic noise-making plot on Earth, another nuclear submarine, the *USS Thresher* SS 593, was on sea trials, and it sank about 300 miles out off of Boston Harbor. It was absolutely one of the most moving days of my life. Dozens of shipyard workers who maybe had never shed a tear in their lives, were openly crying and trembling over this—the most horrible event that could possibly be imagined. Every crewmember was shaken and crying and stunned. Many shipyard types were moved to a point where they hugged every submarine sailor and wished us strength and a safe submarine life and existence.

First our President was assassinated, and now the *Thresher* had sunk. It was a poignant time to reflect and overcome adversities and get our submarine safely through sea trials, to show the world that no disaster was going to sway us from our task. We would make our fallen President and the lost crewmembers of the *USS Thresher* very proud of what we were going to do to celebrate their legacies. We were invigorated and inspired to bring out the best in our submarine—the *USS Nathan Hale* SSBN 623—to be a major spark of positivity in a period of multiple tragedies. And we did.

When we finished our Cape Canaveral portion of our sea trials, we qualified to show off in a rather special way. We tied an inverted broom to our #1 periscope mast and proudly entered Port Canaveral with honor and dignity. The inverted broom image indicated to submariners and to all assembled spectators that we had achieved a clean sweep—all objectives realized. The reaction at the Port Facilities was spectacular. The docks lined up with a cheering and noisy crowd yelling, screaming, and applauding—making those of us onboard the docking sub so very proud. We felt ten feet tall—and invincible. It was a true moment in time that I will never forget.

## 2. Missile Launch Testing

A week prior to our trials, our sister crew, The Blue Crew, had command of the sub, and it was their chance to launch. We, members of the Gold Crew, had the opportunity to ride out to witness their launch on the *OI—Observation Island*. Observing a very sophisticated ship with all of the latest and most complex electronic telemetry equipment available and recording every moment of the launch prior to, during, and track down range to splash down, is quite an awesome thing. It was a beautiful day, and it was an electrically charged feeling that was palpable through the entire launch sequence.

Finally, the moment came, and with the aid of a marker—a very tall pole or stanchion attached to the sail of the submerged sub—the countdown began. 5-4-3-2-1-0—the most magnificent sight appeared—approximately three stories high, 56 inches in diameter—broaching up through the beautiful blue waves and waters a few miles offshore from Cape Canaveral. Suddenly, a Polaris A-1 Missile arose in all its magnificence. This was an experience of a lifetime. We knew we were witnessing a part of

## First Days at Sea

history. Many days and months before, we were in a shipyard with cold, flat HY80 steel being rolled into hull segments to eventually become a submarine.

And so here it was. A Polaris A-1 missile suddenly appeared out of a submarine and broached the surface of the Atlantic Ocean. And in an instant, it suddenly ignited its solid propellant fuel, and, with a mighty roar, the missile streaked skyward. We were at a loss for words to make sense of what had just occurred. The civilians aboard the *OI* and the regular crew of the *OI* treated us submarine crew members with awe. We were very conspicuous because those of us on nuclear subs wore a special coverall called *poopy suit*, because it had a back panel in the back for obvious reasons. Anyway, they looked at us and engaged us like we were rock stars, or, better yet, like we were astronauts! We were to be looked upon and treated specially for the unusual job we were doing and for the amount of peril we would be subjecting ourselves to—to maintain peace around the world.

The Blue Crew's launch was carried out to perfection, but the missile went off-course down range, and the range officer had to push a button to self-destruct the missile. While the Gold Crew missile launch qualified for the inverted broom tradition, The Blue Crew self-destruct call scrubbed their broom salute. Because of the two-crew concept, there would be a constant challenge to show off which was the better crew and which would achieve the greatest triumphs. Of course, every day, the members of the Gold Crew excelled in every way possible. We were good; our counterparts, the Blue Crew, were acceptable. We were synchronized and good to the core; we functioned like a well-tuned machine.

The following day, the joy was somewhat diminished when we were told that a crewmember of the surface ship, the *Observation Island,* had suffered a fatal accident. It seems that this crewmember decided, after a couple of brews, to climb a nearby water tower and take a nap in the cool breezes on high. Sad to say that, during his sleep, he rolled over and took quite a plunge to his death. I almost did not want to write about this incident, but because there was such an irony involved, I have. The young sailor landed approximately where we had created the mock grave of J.P. Riley a week before.

Meanwhile, back on the submarine, one of our ship's cooks, Desidario, managed to catch enough mixed fish breeds, with some fishing line attached to a Coke bottle, to feed the entire crew onboard. Watching Desi manipulate the Coke bottle was amazing. By manipulating his wrist, he could reel in every fish as if he had a Shakespeare-like precision fishing reel—a trick or a talent he had honed growing up in the Philippines. Our commanding officer, Commander Samuel Strong Ellis, allowed this to happen since the senior most Naval officer (SOPA—Senior Officer Present Afloat) at Cape Canaveral was an ardent fisherman himself, and he sanctioned the fish feast—with one contingency. He wanted to be onboard to dine with us. Captain Brown was his name, and quite a unique and unforgettable man he was, as well as a brilliant and humble humanitarian. Captain Brown had the ability to efficiently coordinate the entire Polaris Missile Program Testing Shore Preparation to flow perfectly and as smoothly as possible.

## First Days at Sea

Needless to say, our Gold Crew of the *USS Nathan Hale* SSBNS 623 was trying to exceed beyond our wildest dreams.

### *Story: Some Real R&R*

Next on our travels, we were cleared for a little R&R (rest and relaxation), which was the very first such experience for this brand-new sub and crew. We cruised from Cape Canaveral to Christianstadt in the Virgin Islands—a true tropical paradise. The pier we tied up to was stuck way out into the water, where the water was quite deep. It was so clear that you could see the sandy bottom. Because there was no other sign of life or guards apparent, we had to post our own armed guard to ensure our safety and security. One of my civilian friends who was riding with us had a rent-a-car at his disposal from his parent company, Treadwell—the manufacturer of the Oxygen Generators that had been installed aboard our sub. Since he was unable to use the VW Bug rental, he gave me the keys so I had the use of it.

A few friends and I had the time off, so off we drove. We had two choices—Scenic Route 1 or Route 1. We chose the scenic route. This took us literally into the jungles of the island on a dramatically steep road that took us past many rum manufacturing areas with their visible tall furnaces that were necessary for the production of the rum. Eventually, we came upon a beautiful B&B nestled in the mountainside, only to discover that it was closed for the season. However, when the owner discovered who we were, he uncovered and opened up a scenic deck area within his establishment. Suddenly, we were being treated to the most wonderful welcoming we had ever experienced. The drinks (rum) flowed, and then food appeared, and we had a wonderful time. When we departed, the owner, a Dutch National by the name of Sjord Van Tassel, refused any money from us. It certainly was not what we planned, but we were extremely grateful and thankful for his hospitality.

We departed and finally reached the other side of the island at a town called Frederickstadt. My cash was running low. It was well before the days of carrying credit cards, and I had stuffed a check into my wallet. By that point, when I pulled it out, it looked like hell and not very convincing of its authenticity. I decided to go to a local bank, convinced it would be denied. Instead, when I showed the bank manager my military ID and he knew that I was representing the submarine in Christianstadt, he approved it in a heartbeat. With no questions asked, he wished me a wonderful visit.

Our trip was all very good, and the scenery and people were very special, but we were told to watch out for some revolutionary group that wanted its independence from Holland. After the visit to Frederickstadt, we were tired, so we took the shortest and most direct route back, Route 1—a modern, paved road. At one point, as we approached a tourist destination with all of the bells and whistles of a golf course and resort, we were surprised by a lot of commotion, and we heard gunfire. We managed to get by unscathed, but it seems that the revolutionary group had attacked golfing tourists and killed several. The next day, we heard that six to nine people were found dead. We made haste getting back to the submarine and discovered that we now had company in the waters near

## First Days at Sea

our mooring. A U.S. Destroyer, which coincidentally was in the neighborhood, had been dispatched to back us up if the revolutionaries decided to do something stupid. The rest of our stay was uneventful, and we headed back to the shipyard for Post Sea Trial/Post Missile Launch Testing, the purpose of which was to fix, repair, or tweak all problem areas discovered during our very extensive and inclusive sea trials. We returned to Electric Boat General Dynamics Shipyard very proud of what we had accomplished.

# B. Post-Op Sea Trials

## 1. Welcome Home and Ceremony

Upon entering the shipyard back at Electric Boat General Dynamics in Groton, Connecticut, a massive welcome home scene awaited us with banners, streamers, and a fire boat (a tug with a high-pressure water gun on its bow) sending a stream of water into the air. I might add that, as we approached the shipyard, our Periscope #1 once again had the inverted broom mounted, to the delight of all spectators. And over the extensive loudspeaker system throughout the entire shipyard, "Eternal Father, Strong to Save" could be heard playing loud and clear. Chills ran up and down my spine. Lots of tears of pride and honor were expressed by each and every shipyard worker and especially from those of us, the crew of the *USS Nathan Hale* SSBN 623 Gold. It should be noted that the Blue Crew was a little subdued because they had been unable to achieve "the sweep," i.e., the inverted broom significance. It also has to be noted that the shipyard workers (our yard birds) were filled with pride for what we had accomplished but also for the immense gratification they felt for having built this awesome symbol of freedom.

I realized a long time ago, when I decided to take on this task of writing about my submarine service, that it might possibly become many many volumes because of the unique world of a submariner. For now, I offer this humble beginning. On a daily basis onboard a submarine, one is constantly on his toes doing something to assure everyone's safety and survival. It is truly a life of completing tasks on a minute-to-minute basis to maintain survival and prevent the sub from entering harm's way. In the civilian world, one might expect life-altering situations to occur a fair amount of time in any given year. However, submariners face potential life-altering situations every minute of every day. No disrespect to our civilian friends and neighbors, but there is a decided difference.

## 2. LCU System—Life Change Unit System

The Navy went as far as directing a detailed study of stress that all Naval personnel encounter during their long deployments all over the world. The intention of the study was to come up with a formula for detecting *who*, on an individual basis, might be on the verge of breaking due to emotional distress. The study took more than eight years of scientific brainstorming and testing to create the LCU System—LCU or Life Change Unit. This system placed a numeric value for the experiences of a sailor in his normal routine such as: moving from one Naval command to another (with or without family); separation from family; long deployments; different types of problems back home; working

## First Days at Sea

with explosives, weaponry, etc. The list of possible day-to-day encounters was extensive, and each was scientifically given a number value proven to be a fair measuring stick to assess someone's mental condition for a military task-at-hand. Each and every daily encounter was given a numeric value, and each was considered a Life Change Unit.

I'll make it short. The system worked well for the members of the surface Navy and was used extensively. As long as a sailor did not exceed 30 LCUs, he was fine, and this was widely accepted throughout the Navy and for years was a time-tested tool that functioned well. However! The day finally came when they decided—unwisely—to use this time-tested scientific method on submariners, and it was a mind-boggling disaster. The rule was, if a sailor exceeded 30 LCUs in any given year, he would be counseled, and steps were taken to help the individual to relieve him or her of their stress.

Now, when the submariner enters the picture, a disaster of untold proportions occurs instantly. The multi-million-dollar system was then literally shit-canned! And it had to be erased and denied that it ever existed. Why? Simply put, when this LCU System was administered to a submariner, each and every submariner exceeded 30 LCUs in and on every single day! Question—how can you run a Nuclear Power Submarine Navy if the LCU System was applied? Within days the entire LCU organization was disbanded, and all reference material disappeared. What followed was a reassessment of additional submarine manifest to start including taking on medical doctors, clergymen, and psychologists—hoping that if any need arose, there would be someone onboard to help. The fact is that, as time went on, all of these medical and clerical professionals were slowly, but surely, phased out. The submariners proved to be unique individuals, and in my twenty-plus years, I can assuredly attest to this. I can draw a parallel with submariners to every Navy pilot who has landed onboard an aircraft carrier, and that is maximum stress and strain exerted on a human being during wartime and peace.

The mental acuity and the ability to make life-altering, split-second decisions, to say the least, should be readily apparent to one and all—civilian or military. A stray thought has just popped into my pea brain. These words will be a different angle altogether. Submariners were credited with many extraordinary feats in World War II. One special deed was the recovery of downed pilots, including George W. Bush, a future President of the United States of America. Additionally, the early Frogman deployments from submarines, as well as our current SEAL Teams' covert deployments to highly tenuous situations all over the world, are other examples. I mention this only to stress the point that, in each case, the entire crew of a submarine (and the submarine itself) become totally exposed and vulnerable to all kinds of mayhem. All submariners—brothers, sons, fathers, and uncles are always acutely aware of their own mortality, but each and every one carries on with great pride and awareness, doing what we do gladly for God and country. And, of course, now there are many courageous women serving on submarines, too.

After the submarine *USS Nathan Hale* returned to Electric Boat General Dynamics for our post sea trial and extensive sea trial, we were entering a phase of repairing, tweaking, and

## First Days at Sea

general deep review of any malfunctions that had cropped up during the extensive at-sea testing. Thank God we had no major problems, but we did uncover a lot of nit-node issues that needed to be dealt with in an efficient manner.

## Story: A Little Diversion

Despite the far-reaching post-op workload, I was able to get some time off, and off I went again to visit my mother and father, and to see some friends and acquaintances, which, of course, included my ex-girlfriend, Ann, and her parents. It was summer, and she was home from college, which made for a wonderful visit that included taking Ann and her sister, Emma, for a motorcycle ride. I mention that, because, in writing this, I cannot prevent my memories of happiness at being part of Ann's family and everything we had shared together enter my consciousness again. Soon thereafter Ann's parents moved to another city, but as the years went by, I was drawn many times to their old house and the precious memories I had locked away in my memory banks.

Over the years, and I am talking about *many* years, I would find time to go back home to visit, to relive those memories once again. When I got back to Yonkers, I would automatically drive to Morsemere Avenue and park near Ann's old house, dwell on the past, and think of sweet nothings. What if we had stayed together? What if we had stayed together and gotten married? All of these thoughts remained in a special place in my mind forever—a special place where I could go during times of trouble and stress. This was the special place in my mind reserved for the happy times I'd experienced with Ann. And my world would be right again.

Now let me throw out a teaser to you. Do you know what might happen forty-eight years later? How about a book written and tons of friends reunited!? Let that float around in your brain for a while. I will fill you in sometime in the future. Right now, I have to get back to Electric Boat General Dynamics to supervise my portion of the Post-Op Sea Trial adventure.

---

I have to say, when you experience everything surrounding a shipyard and dwell there as long as I and my fellow submariners had, you wonder how in the hell a sophisticated, complex nuclear submarine could come out of all this madness and mayhem. Fact is, throughout all of this seemingly endless disarray is a deep-seated focus to achieve the best and to perfect the best submarine that has ever been built.

This Post-Op Shipyard period went extremely well, and the sub was entering a new phase. With the Blue Crew in command of the sub and under orders to take it to the Naval Weapons Station in Charleston, South Carolina, we of the Gold Crew made a monumental move to set up our off-crew office in Charleston as well. That meant every crewmember, including all married men, had to move their families and personal belongings to Charleston and set up housekeeping there. We single guys had a little easier time of it, being far less encumbered.

# C. Charleston, South Carolina

## 1. My Arrival

The day arrived when I flew to Charleston, South Carolina, to start this non-shipyard, serious submarine life, which meant loading out the missile tubes with nuclear-tipped missiles and loading nuclear-tipped torpedoes and non-nuclear torpedoes. There were other ordnances that suddenly made one realize that you were going to be operating onboard a very lethal weapon-of-war and that the days in the shipyard were really a picnic. The reality of it was that I would be living alongside weapons that so far exceeded all of the explosives used in every war that had ever been fought. It was a sobering thought. All of this on just one submarine.

My trip to Charleston, South Carolina, was quite an eye-opener. I flew in and was shocked when the pilot and co-pilot hustled around to open the fuselage and exited the plane on some rickety makeshift stairs that looked pretty unsafe. Back to that scene in a minute. I have to mention what hit me as the fuselage door was opened. An odor flooded into the plane—horrible to say the least, when it is your first experience smelling anything like it. It was the exhaust of the paper mill—foul and pungent.

At the bottom of the stairs was an old gentleman manning a rather large fire extinguisher, which literally dwarfed him. I had serious doubts that, if he had to use it, he would have a terrible time of it. He was the total Charleston ground crew—there to cover any and all emergencies. Off in the near distance. I spotted what looked to be a fruit-and-vegetable stand, i.e., extensive tables with strings of what looked to be temporary lights.

Backing up again. Besides the odor from the paper mill, the ambient temperature was in the high 90s, and the humidity was 100%. So, the smell, the temperature, and the humidity were quite a shock to my system.

Our pilot and co-pilot were now stripped to their white dress shirts; out of necessity, it seemed, they were now baggage handlers, emptying the baggage storage and putting all items on old-fashioned railroad pushcarts. Once the carts were loaded and pushed over to what I had perceived to be a fruit-and-vegetable stand, that now became the baggage reclaim area. My first half hour in Charleston, South Carolina, was actually like entering a time warp or a third-world country experience.

## Story: Boiled Peanuts

Following this scene, a true caricature of a person approached me and, in his Charlestonian drawl, offered his cab and services.

## First Days at Sea

I carried my seabag, and off we went, heading for the first time to the Naval Base Charleston. As we drove through miles of wooded terrain, the taxicab driver offered me a variety of pills and drugs. I felt like the level of sophistication I thought I had developed over the course of my young life had not prepared me for this moment. Me—a New Yorker with many experiences under my belt (so I thought!) was completely at a loss for words. I stuttered and stammered, spouting out a shocked "NO, thank you." That was all I could muster up. He didn't push the issue any further, and I was relieved. Soon after, this character offered me a handful of what he called "boiled peanuts." I was in my dress whites uniform, so I grabbed the soggy mess to prevent soiling my uniform. This was not a pleasant moment for me, but I did become intrigued and curious. I told him that, where I came from, if we get our peanuts in the shell wet, we throw them away. He merely insisted that I try them. "Try them; you'll like them," he kept repeating. I maneuvered one and managed to not make a mess. I tasted these warm, soggy, salty gems, and I totally fell in love with them. And to this day, I still love them.

—⚍—

We eventually made it to a very well-used area outside of the United States Naval Base at Charleston, South Carolina. The main drag is called Reynolds Avenue, which consisted of an overabundance of drinking establishments. There were approximately fifty of them. And on some of the side streets, there were another fifteen or twenty more of these establishments. Back in the day, the enlisted types were not paid very well, no matter what service you were in—Navy, Army, Air Force, or Coast Guard. Very few servicemen had automobiles, so they were limited to a social life that kept everyone on base, frequenting the Enlisted Club or the Acey Deucey Club. The Enlisted Club was for enlisted men up to 3rd class. The 2nd class and first class had their own club—the Acey Deucey. Two other clubs also existed, and they were the Chiefs' Club and the Officers' Club.

## 2. The Strip

But the preferred drinking spots were just outside the main gate, better known as the "Strip." And I do believe—actually I know for sure—this was a unique phenomenon outside of Naval Bases due to the extremely large number of sailors packed onboard the many ships and submarines in port. Because of the numerous bars, many of the bars were adopted by a ship, or in our case, our submarine crew. Twenty-five cents for a cab from the barracks to the front gate and two to three dollars to be part of the circus at each bar you entered—25 cents for canned beer and plenty of barmaids of all shapes and sizes. Adding to that were many bizarre personalities and rampant testosterone, making for plenty of sexual activity, sometimes in the corners of the drinking establishments.

A friend and I decided to visit one bar in particular—a known lowlife joint. As we walked up to the bar to order a beer, a sailor next to us was also trying to get the barmaid's attention; however, she was carrying on with some of her fellow barmaids and was essentially ignoring her job. The sailor then realized that the barmaids were very intrigued with playing with a tree frog. He somehow staggered over to the barmaid cluster and reached out and grabbed the frog and tossed it into his mouth and swallowed it. He promptly then shouted, "Now can I have a fucking beer!" The girls immediately hopped to it; bar service was restored, and we all got our beers.

Before we exited that joint, I needed to use the head. Remember these joints were never laid out with any architectural blueprints, so wherever anything fit, that's where it was placed. The jukebox was in a peculiar position, and it was not against a wall. So, there was space behind it back near the dark passage where the facilities were located. As I approached the jukebox, I noticed another sailor behind the box, and, as I got closer, I realized a barmaid was on her knees giving him a proper blow job. I merely walked past them and never disturbed them at all. And after I finished my business and walked past them again, they were still at it, apparently having a grand old time. Not all of the joints allowed that kind of debauchery, but plenty of milder forms of sexual encounters occurred that were not quite as out-and-out blatant.

—◊—

## Story: The Rose Room

Eventually the Gold Crew of the *USS Nathan Hale* determined that our favorite drinking spot was The Rose Room, and it became our hangout. It was owned by I.B. Lee and his wife, Bell. I.B. and Bell did not allow any outrageous behavior in their establishment. Eventually I learned that I.B. and his mother were part of the underworld of the Strip, and that I.B.'s mother, Hillary, was the female Don of the Strip as well as the matron in control of all of the barmaids. Hillary owned and operated a large bar located in the middle of the Strip that was an ancient old Victorian house in the middle of all of the bars that were constructed out of cinder blocks and were only one story high.

Hillary's bar was a full three-story building, which included a stairway up to a large porch and the entryway to the reconfigured, once-elegant parlor that became the barroom. And upstairs at this establishment is where all the barmaids lived—albeit in squalid conditions. None of these young women lived away from the Strip. Their diets consisted mainly of bar food—and I don't mean hamburgers. They consumed pickled pig's feet, pickled eggs, and packaged snacks of peanuts and potato chips from the clip strips. Sometimes sailors would bring some real food to a favorite barmaid. I have to remind you that all of this is accurate and true. This was the south in the early sixties. Most of the south really looked more like a third-world country, and the Civil War was still being talked about in a passionate way.

---

I promise you we will get back to the submarine narrative, but you have to hear about some of these side stories. I had broken away from the Strip. I met a young lady, and we started

## First Days at Sea

dating. Her father took a liking to me, and, when he heard I was going to buy a car, he offered to help. He was a medical doctor, and he was getting ready to sell his 1961 Cadillac Coupe DeVille. He listened to my plan for a purchase but insisted that his car, with very low mileage, would be a smarter purchase. So, I became the proud owner of a 1961 Cadillac—jet black with full red-leather upholstery and headliner, and all of the amenities I would ever want or need. My dating days with Doctor Smith's daughter were soon over when she discovered she was pregnant by her previous gentleman friend. I was out of there quickly!

Life went on, and I visited the Strip occasionally, but I spent more of my time off going to the beach and seeing some of the sights of Charleston—historic plantations, forts, etc.

One day, however, as I was visiting The Rose Room, I.B. approached me and told me he had a proposition for me. I can tell you now that what I am about to relay to you is true—I swear to God. I.B. said that, since I had a bigger car than he owned, he would like to take a road trip with me—completely at his expense—to go and "buy some girls." Yes, he said, "Buy. Some. Girls!" Here I was, the sophisticated New York boy, trying to digest what I was hearing. I had the time on my hands, so I accepted this strange undertaking. Soon thereafter, we were on the road, and I.B. took me into Scarlet O'Hara/*Gone with the Wind*/Tara parts of South Carolina—where time had stopped.

In this era, young biracial offspring were stigmatized and were not accepted by blacks or whites, but instead were used by many whites as prostitutes in brothels and at the notorious "fish camps." These camps were located far into the woods and were very secluded, where fishing, drinking, and fucking were on the main menu. As I.B. directed my driving here and there, I sat drinking a beer or two and watched one shocking scene after another, which caused me to shudder way down deep inside of me.

I.B. literally bought three biracial girls. In those days, these girls were known as mulattoes—considered a rather offensive term today. They carried no belongings with them, and they seemed to be unfazed about being driven off by a stranger. We headed back to Charleston. These girls were not ugly. They were attractive in their own way. I.B. gave each girl a brown paper bag, the contents of which were a comb, a brush, a toothbrush and toothpaste, and lipstick. Sitting in the car, the girls opened their bag and pulled out these items one by one. Now the shocker is that none of the girls knew what any of these things were and what they were used for. This ain't no bullshit! One of the girls started brushing her eyebrows with the toothbrush. It was unreal. All I could think was, "Oh, my God, these young ladies were born and raised for carnal pleasure and to be totally managed and controlled for their entire lives."

We drove back to Charleston and arrived at I.B.'s mother's Victorian mansion/bar/barmaids' barracks. The girls were barely introduced to Hillary before they were hustled off upstairs. The next time I saw any one of these girls was in one of the bars on the Strip, where I watched as she persuaded a young naïve sailor to buy a bottle of champagne—at a very inflated price. Yes, many drunken sailors get stupid as they get inebriated. These bottles were called "splits" around the

## First Days at Sea

world, but in Charleston they were called "thumpers," because when they were empty, the thick glass bottle would quite often be utilized to "thump" a drunken sailor who had become unmanageable.

I have to clarify one point here. The vast majority of the sailors frequenting these joints were non-submarine types. The surface-craft Navy was huge, and the submarine types' pay scale was quite different. Submariners' pay was almost double that of surface sailors, with hazardous-duty pay, proficiency pay, and other benefits. This allowed the submarine types to venture away from the Strip, therefore, many of us avoided being relegated to just the bars on the Strip. I spent my share of time on the Strip with my fellow submariners, but it was more for the spectacle and outrageous goings-on and to watch the animals at play.

For example, at one bar, a large-statured barmaid delivered two bottles of beer to a table. She lifted her blouse to reveal two rather large breasts—fully exposed. As she lifted one breast at a time, she revealed a bottle of beer under each and deposited the beer on the table. Then she walked around the back of one of the seated sailors and placed one breast on each of his shoulders. It was absolutely a sight—with his head in the middle of two gigantic breasts. Wish I had a camera.

At another local bar/joint, I witnessed this scene. In a darkened area toward the back of the establishment, a young lady sat spread-eagle on a pool table with a sailor giving her a "beef injection"—obviously trying to cure her of some terrible disease. The look on her face afterward and her broad smile,

I guess, indicated that she was cured and fully recovered. I must have witnessed a miracle.

As mentioned previously, Charleston was, in my estimation, more like a third-world nation back in the 1960s. The old way of doing things still dominated what was accepted and what was not. For example, Charleston had scores of red-light districts, and they blatantly displayed a red bulb dangling off the length of wire from their sign—a clear indication that this was a brothel. The famous Market Street in downtown Charleston, which is today visited by a million-plus tourists each year, was the most concentrated whorehouse location in all of South Carolina. It looked like Christmas decorative lights—all red, as far as the eye could see.

One day while cruising around North Charleston, I spotted some construction activity. What aroused my curiosity, however, was the strategic tree cutting going on. The trees were being cut to a certain height, and, instead of removing the stumps, certain stumps were mapped out in a pattern. Unbelievably (to me at least), these stumps became the foundation for the modest home that would be erected on the site.

Cows and chickens were a common sight, as well as many '50s-era cars and trucks, as seen in Cuba today. The streets of Charleston, South Carolina, were lined with them. Every other vehicle contained occupants driving and drinking with a highly visible can of beer in hand. And it was all legal because the bottle or the can was in a brown paper bag. White lightning liquor could be bought in many locales, with the biggest sales occurring on Sundays. That was because of the Blue Laws still on the books—ancient laws that prevented booze from being

## First Days at Sea

sold on Sunday. Another Blue Law allowed a man to relieve himself in public—for example, if a farmer was plowing his field and had to pee, he could relieve himself right there instead of walking to a tree line for cover or discreetness.

All of what I've described was real, but just imagine the contrast—a mere 50 feet away, behind a rather long fence and Marine Gate Guards, was a sophisticated Naval Base with the most technologically advanced and engineered United States Navy ships and submarines. Talk about a time warp or a contrast.

## 3. Fleet Ballistic Missile Submarine Training Center

Let's get back to the submarine world. The nuclear submarine was in its infancy, but its importance was reflected in the fact that an entire section of the base, formerly a neglected and wooded area, was completely transformed into a little city unto itself. The focal point of this area was a brand-new building called the Fleet Ballistic Missile Submarine Training Center, which housed the duplication of all of the systems onboard a submarine in a brick-and-mortar building—missile tube, torpedo tube, engineering, and electrical and electronic systems for off-crew refresher training. The only thing missing was a nuclear reactor!

In addition to the main building, new barracks, new chow hall, new commissary, Navy Exchange, barber shop, optometry shop, and a Navy Credit Union Branch were also constructed—all brand new and state of the art. We also had a new office building to maintain the administrative business when we were in our off-crew status.

For clarification and refresher purposes, each Fleet Ballistic Missile Submarine has two crews—the Gold Crew and the Blue Crew. The submarine is continuously deployed except for thirty-day upkeeps. During these upkeeps, there is a change-of-command and a change of crew from the Gold Crew to the Blue Crew, and vice versa. The relief crew would make repairs necessary and re-provision and then depart for patrol anywhere from fifty to sixty days of deployment. Sometimes, however, our deployment would have to be extended because a sister sub that would be relieving us in that patrol zone might experience a technical or engineering problem, and we would have to cover for the zone and/or targets assigned to that ailing sub until their deployment problems were resolved, which necessarily added considerably more time at sea, stretching thin our onboard supplies. The problems that ensued on the sub were usually few, but certain situations could present monumental dilemmas. For instance, smoking was quite prevalent on the subs, and extended patrols meant many of us would run out of cigarettes. That was devastating to any submariner.

Our Gold Crew flew back to Charleston and started our off-crew period. The first thirty days consisted of rest and recuperation. The next period was Refresher Training at the Fleet Ballistic Missile Submarine Training Center—FBMSTC. This became our ongoing cycle of crew changes, patrol deployments, fly home for R&R with family, refresher training, fly back to relieve the Blue Crew. And that cycle continued on. Our routine proved to be very successful, and the crew's

## First Days at Sea

proficiency was never in doubt. Our mission was always well-planned and quite achievable. The main success of all successes was *deterrence* during the days of the Cold War. Our enemies around the world knew that we were on patrol and invisible. Our silent service was very capable of destroying them if they tried to attack our country and interfere with our way of life.

# Part Three

# First Patrol

# A. Rota, Spain

The day finally arrived. We, the members of the Gold Crew, broke down our off-crew office, boxed up our administrative and medical records, headed to the Charleston Air Force Base, and boarded planes for our flight to Rota, Spain. We split the crews into two groups; the theory was that, if a plane should meet a terrible fate, only half of the crew would be lost. Our captain traveled on one, plane and the executive officer flew on the other plane. Now remember, back in the day, one could approach a machine and buy flight insurance dispensed at many locations in all airports ($2 for a $50,000 payoff.) Since there were two planes, many of my cohorts bought insurance for crewmembers on the other plane and vice versa. I could never bring myself to participate, or think about the jinx factor, and I thank God there never has been a policy fulfilled.

We finally landed safely in Rota, Spain, where the USA had an agreement to outfit an airbase and port facilities. We rode

## Real Stories from a Nuclear Submariner

buses down to the port and moved onboard the submarine tender *USS Canopus*. This vessel was literally a floating city with every capability to support itself and other submarines that might tie up next to it. Submarine tenders were floating shipyards, capable of executing major and minor repairs. Many talented sailors skillfully serviced every need of the submarines alongside. In my opinion, these ships will never be glorified in a feature film, but they should be.

The interior of these mighty vessels stored nuclear and conventional torpedoes, Polaris Missiles, and every small arm in service, as well as tons of ammunition. Additionally, there were machine shops, periscope shops, electronic repair shops, a hospital, dental office, post office, and a chaplain's office. Simply put, our every need and desire could be met or exceeded.

The Blue Crew took the *Nathan Hale* on its first patrol after departing CONUS (Continental United States) and sixty days later was due to surface and enter the U.S. Base in Rota, Spain. At mid-day those of us on the Gold Crew manned the rails, watching our beautiful sub under tow, and soon it would be nestled in its berth up against the tender. Eventually, after the necessary checks and inspections eliminating any toxic or nuclear radiation readings, the brow (gangway) was opened, and we proceeded onboard to meet and greet and hear stories about their exploits—many good stories that Tom Clancy would love to feature in a movie. But these stories will never be told, as they are still too sensitive and revealing. Seeing our Blue Crew counterparts was a great experience. Having been

## First Patrol

submerged for sixty days, they appeared pale and colorless, but they were in great spirits.

The Gold Crew then moved onboard into our respective specialty areas and began our change-of-command. We got the information needed to understand where problems existed and corrective measures were required. In three days, the Gold Crew would take over the command of the *Nathan Hale*. We watched our Blue Crew members, finally in proper uniform of the day, depart to fly home and reunite with their loved ones. Upon their departure, we moved onboard the sub (lock, stock, and barrel) and commenced a thirty-day upkeep, repair, and testing to prepare for our departure and begin our first patrol.

We swapped missiles, torpedoes, and many repair parts. After preparing to take on provisions and medical needs, we left the tender for a two-day sea trial. We then entered the port and tied up to the tender for final fixes and supplies before departing on patrol. Our first patrol was significant because we carried a Catholic priest, a psychologist, a full-fledged doctor, and lastly, two technical representatives to cover some top-secret gadgets onboard.

Our departure was low-key because we knew that the Russians had observation ships nearby monitoring us. Because of our state-of-the-art construction, we dove and rode silent, confusing them on our location and heading. Their subs were constructed in haste, with many corners cut. Consequently, a Russian sub sounded like a freight train underwater. Our construction, on the other hand, was early stealth in practice. All mounted machinery and decks were shock-mounted with rubber cushions or pads. Our submarine had a near-zero sound signature compared to the Russians'. We had the capability of tailing a Russian sub and literally could hear everyday activities onboard their subs. This could be doors opening and closing or loud voices, so if someone raised his voice, we could hear it. Our mission was to be silent and run deep in complete secrecy to achieve our deterrent purpose.

Our CO was Commander Samuel Strong Ellis. His onboard title was "Captain." Soon after getting underway, Captain Ellis opened up his orders and read them. After sharing this information with the rest of the officers onboard, he headed to the control room to speak to the entire submarine crew over the 1MC communication system. In an exuberant voice, he said, "This is your Captain," followed by, "Underway on Nuclear Power." He then told the crew our objectives and where we were headed. Of course, there were some things that he could not share. We were now initiating our daily routine, which was based only on our clocks and watches, with absolutely no reliance on sunrises or sunsets.

## Story: First Visit to Downtown Rota, Spain

It was easy to settle in because the crew was tired and exhausted from working hard during our thirty-day refit. Our onboard cycle was six hours on duty—or *watch*—and twelve hours off. However, I have to back up a little and cover some of my first visit to downtown Rota, Spain. Before we were allowed to make this trip, our entire crew had to listen to a lecture about the *do's and don'ts* while on sovereign Spanish soil. We

## First Patrol

found it odd that we were told to drink booze, wine, and beer, but that we were not to drink the local water or eat the food because bacteria levels were high, especially in the fish, since all raw sewage was piped into Rota Harbor by all municipalities around the bay. So, did you get the point? Drink to your heart's content, and you'd better eat onboard before going on liberty in town. Also, there was another major point to reckon with. Dictator Franco had three different police forces, but the one to fear and stay clear of was called *The Guardia Seville*. They had an attitude and a license to kill.

The Guardia and our U.S. Marines had their own separate gates. When we left the base, our Marines would check our IDs and wave us on. About fifty feet further on, we approached the Guardia's gate, which was manned by two or three of their kind, wearing very sharp-looking uniforms. On each of their heads was a patent-leather wide-brimmed hat with the back portion of the brim bent up against the back of the cap. There were no smiles, no cordial greetings—just stares of intimidation. After being waved through, we approached the downtown area, where ten or fifteen bars appeared and not much else. I felt like I was in, or on, a Mexican film set—waiting for John Wayne to come up on a horse.

Passing one adobe joint after another, we settled on one called Loco El Gotto, or Crazy Cat. The interior was quite a surprise. It was picturesque and very nice, and to our amazement, it was air-conditioned. After much beer and rum was consumed, a huge hunger came over me. One of the barmaids brought out a plate of paella for herself. The aroma was infectious. Even though we were warned not to eat local food, I managed to order some for myself. I wanted to lick the plate clean—it was so damned good. The fact is that, to my knowledge, no illness occurred. My friends and I felt like we were an early episode of Anthony Bourdain.

After a relaxing time in town and still able to navigate back to the sub, we approached the gate to the base; the Spanish guards were having a rough time with an unruly dog that looked, and was acting, menacingly. One of the Guardia Seville took his automatic rifle off of his shoulder and fired an automatic burst of bullets into the dog—not a pretty sight. He then pushed the carcass into a ditch nearby. By the time we reached the gate, we were all stone sober and on our best behavior—and we had a story to tell our friends back onboard the sub.

---

One week later, a few of us took a cab to a town called Puerto. Its full name was El Puerto de Santa Maria, and it was from here that Christopher Columbus launched his first cruise to the New World—consequently naming one of his ships the *Santa Maria*. We went to a bullfight, and the Spaniards treated us like rock stars, even sharing their wine, which was carried in a leather kidney-shaped canteen called a *bota*. It was a wonderful, warm experience. We were in our military uniforms, so we were very prominent, and we stood out like sore thumbs. When we left the arena, we continued to frequent many bars because they sporadically served *topas* (bar snacks) of many different types. Each *topas* was a culinary delight—fish, crustaceans, cheese, veggies, and meats. To my liking, the American *topas* served stateside are a poor representation of what we experienced in Spain.

## Story: International Incident Averted

Bouncing from bar to bar and experiencing each bar's ambiance was great until we realized that we were getting seriously drunk. Our little group got separated, and my plan was to head back to the sub. It was late in the day, and I was not too coherent. I found myself heading out of town on foot, with no logical plan. The sun was down, and I was totally lost and confused. Suddenly it was dark—with no moonlight at all. A car or two passed me by, but I was ignored. All of a sudden—and "this ain't no bullshit"—a truck went by and came to a screeching halt. I recognized the uniform of the Guardia Seville screaming at me to "Alto! Alto!" But I panicked and ran. They had no flashlights. I was soon over the side of the road—stumbling and in total fear for my life! I was imagining gunfire and bullets whizzing past me. However, I soon realized they were real, and in complete darkness, I ran off the shoulder of the road down an embankment to unwittingly face my first encounter with a cactus.

Cactus is used as fencing to separate parcels of land. I ran smack dab into one cactus barrier after another and literally waded through a stream or two. After passing another cactus, I finally realized that the Guardia had given up looking for this drunken sailor. I was regaining my senses and realized my jumper top had many many cactus needles stuck in the canvas material, so I painfully took the jumper off and discarded it. I was too drunk to care. Eventually I found a main road, and the sailors' adage of "God takes care of drunks and sailors" came true for me! Still staggering a bit, a car came by, and even though I was still drunk, I thought that the Guardia had come back for me. Instead, the car came to a halt, and a guy came to my rescue. He was a sailor stationed on the tender. His wife also came to my aid, and they walked me to their car. They turned around with me in the car, and we headed back to the Navy base. The wife actually sat in the back seat with me, as I sat with just my pants and shoes on—topless and covered in cactus needles, blood, and mud. She put her hand behind my head for support and started plucking cactus needles from my torso. I was then sober enough to ask her why they decided to stop. She said that they recognized me as being a U.S. sailor, because, throughout my self-inflicted ordeal, my wallet was still lopped over my waistband. Only U.S. sailors made this a time-tested method of carrying a wallet. Why I had not lost it in my trek, I will never know—God takes care of drunks and sailors!

Sometime later I found myself onboard the tender in the sickbay area, sitting on a stainless-steel swivel stool with two or three Navy corpsmen plucking many cactus needles from my body—stopping from time to time to sweep up the dropped needles and start again. At one point I was taken to a shower, and I managed to do a half-assed job of cleaning myself off—finding more needles that were hidden by dirt or blood or mud. It was painful, to say the least. I was then directed back to the stool, and a second round of plucking

## First Patrol

began. Hours later, I was released and allowed to go back to the sub. The laughter was loud and the comments and joking relentless, as I settled into the routine on the boat. One thing was for sure. A pair of tweezers was always nearby.

And my new nickname became *Needles*—the guy with the prickly personality! After a few days passed, a story floated around the base that La Guardia, on the same night of my exploits, shot at some unknown character near Puerto. This confirmed to me that I indeed had been shot at—a new meaning of life overwhelmed me! You have to understand that the black market has been, and still is, a major problem throughout Europe. Illegal goods were being smuggled ashore around the Bay of Cadiz every day. Puerto was on the Bay, and Guardia shot indiscriminately at anyone they suspected of being part of it. Cigarettes were the biggest money-making product, followed by illegal immigration.

Back to me and my new enlightenment. Soon I became a focal point. The hour had arrived when I was requested to sit down with my CO, Commander Sam Ellis, to have a heart-to-heart about my exploits that night. Now he was known to enjoy a drink or two quite often. He asked me to his stateroom. After some pleasantries, he got down to business, and, instead of asking questions, he simply told me, "To avert any international incident, you will never attempt to relay a detailed sequence of your exploits. If there were shots fired, you were not aware of any incident other than the wild incident being rumored around the submarine base. La Guardia was pursuing a black marketer. Now let's get this submarine prepared to go to sea." On my way out of the Captain's stateroom, he invited me to have a drink with him that night at the Officers' Club. I was anxious, but relieved, to say the least.

At the club later that night, Captain Ellis wanted to hear the actual story, and he laughed like hell. He said it would be in a book he planned to write many years later. Since he was so enamored of my story, I embellished it a bit more by describing how my cohorts in crime had abandoned me. First of all, my good friend Bobby Jankila had to be dragged away from a whorehouse because he insisted on following through on his desire to service every whore in that establishment with his tongue! Navy Shore Patrol had to take him fighting back to the sub in a drunken stupor. And Rat Wallace, the third leg of our ill-fated excursion, found another unique way of getting back to the sub. Rat Wallace passed out in a church, and the priest loaded him up onto a donkey-drawn cart and took him back to the base. Also, after we drank all of the rum the bar had to offer, we switched to cognac and Coke. At that stage, you could have put kerosene and Coke in front of us, and we would never have noticed. Captain Sam Ellis was entertained and became quite relaxed, which was hard to do for any captain of a nuclear submarine at that stage of any refit. Not another word was ever spoken again about Puerto.

# B. Preparations for Patrol

Back to the sub. We were ready to get underway on patrol. Our trip would include Doctor Ross, Father Brown, and psychologist, Doctor Wired—eventually and justifiably called Dr. Weird. Two additional civilians were also onboard for some James Bond top-secret gadgetry testing.

All hands not on watch manned the *daisy chain*. Pallets of fresh veggies, fruit, canned goods, packaged goods, and paper products, intermingled with repair parts, were hoisted onboard. From topside to all points in the sub, one could see a continuous lineup of men handing off item after item (restricted by its size that would fit down the hatch) in all directions until it reached its destination all over the submarine. Every nook and cranny onboard the sub seemed to have something stuffed into it.

I have to interject something here. Probably the most important item of all of the tens of thousands of items brought onboard—perhaps the most important of all—was TOILET

PAPER. Yes, that item has ruined many a submariner's career. Yes, toilet paper. Many years ago, this particular item, which used to be controlled by the senior ship's cook, now was given to the Chief of the Boat, the COB. Because this item was almost as important as the weapons we carried onboard, special attention was paid to it, and a specific *t.p. guru* had to be designated. And the COB sweated about this responsibility because heads, or his head, would roll, if we ever ran out. Shitty story, you say? Remember the toilet-paper hoarding during the pandemic? Fact is, if politicians would include the assurance that "You will never run out of toilet paper while I'm in office," he would get all of the *anal-retentive* voters and win his election handily.

We were then completely outfitted and ready to go out to sea on our first patrol. A final hull inspection, superstructure hand-over-hand thorough inspection, and finally the mile-long checklist was concluded. The nuclear reactor that was in *cold iron mode* was painstakingly, step-by-step activated and brought online. Shore power and all other external utilities were disengaged, and all onboard necessities were then totally supported by our nuclear reactor. With a gentle pull, a support tugboat eased us away from the sub tender, and, once we were in unobstructed waters, the tug was cast off, and the Captain had the helm. He picked up the 1MC and announced fore and aft, "Underway on nuclear power, and God Bless America."

To feel the slight shudder of vibration indicating that we were finally underway and that our very serious purpose was now at hand was intoxicating. Many of us onboard had a

## First Patrol

special tear or two in our eyes, realizing who we were and in what we were about to engage.

As we headed to our dive site, the usual predictable Russian electronic surveillance *Picket Ship* was on standby to monitor our departure. I felt sorry for my Russian counterparts on the Picket cruising around in circles for months at a time to witness another stealthy U.S. submarine slide by with no, or very little, usable sound signature. We proceeded to our dive site at the 100-fathom curve—well away from shore and many miles away from the Picket Ship.

With a due-west course and beyond the 100-fathom curve, the Captain announced over the 1MC, "Dive. Dive. Make your depth 300 feet." Achieving the ordered depth, everyone onboard checked every hull-fitting and every nook and cranny onboard for leaks and any other abnormalities. The Captain then read the part of our underway orders and clarified our mission. It was an exciting moment, and sometimes a chill would run up and down my spine. This was the real deal—not Tom Clancy and his book *Red October*. It was our living book—the *USS Nathan Hale* SSBN 623G. It was reality, and all of us onboard were not on a Hollywood soundstage. We were submariners in *Davy Jones's Locker*. All one hundred and forty-five of us onboard were in a do-or-die situation for the next fifty-five or sixty-five days.

Our routine was quickly established, and, for the off-watch crewmembers it was kip time, which meant that you crawled into your rack and crashed until you were awakened for your watch cycle. Then it was off to the chow hall to have a wonderful dining experience. I have never had a bad meal onboard a submarine in all of the thousands of meals I was privy to experience.

# C. Life Onboard

*I* arrived at my watch station, i. e., the watch in the middle level of the missile compartment on the starboard side called the Launch Control Center. My responsibilities included monitoring sixteen missiles in tubes and all systems in the missile compartment to facilitate the launch of each missile. It was a restricted area, where you couldn't have a shit-shooting contest, otherwise known as social gatherings. A log book was maintained, and every action, incident, or routine maintenance procedure was recorded.

I had a roving watch to aid me. He had the freedom to rove all three levels of the compartment on a constant patrol, monitoring visually all that I could not possibly see. He also controlled a tape recorder in the upper level of the missile compartment that supplied my watch station with music—a lot. My biggest hope was that the rover had the same taste in music as me.

My rover was T.T. Reid (Thorneal Thadeus Reid), and our musical tastes were very compatible; however, I loved to pick on him by constantly playing devil's advocate. In other words, I always replied to his remarks by being contrary and taking the opposite view. That always irritated him to some mild degree. He knew what I was doing, and he would shrug it off as we both laughed together. On one watch cycle, T.T. put a Lou Rawls tape on (reel-to-reel). Now I loved Lou Rawls. T.T. came to my watch station and sat with me for a while as we listened to the tape. Before he had a chance to say anything, I blurted out, "I love this man. Pat Boone is so great. I could listen to him all day long!" T.T. exploded and told me to "fuck off." He stormed off, and I never saw him again that watch cycle. After that, T.T. turned off the tape recorder, so my toying with him backfired on me. We had lots of little jousting matches during the entire patrol and many good laughs, which became diversions to pass the long, lonely, but luckily boring, patrols.

Meanwhile in the Torpedo Room, one of the Old Salts that I mentioned back at Dam Neck, Virginia, Missile Launcher School (beer on bumper), J.P. Riley, was on the verge of losing his cool. In the Torpedo Room, he was confined to such a small space from which he could not leave, and consequently, music became very important to him. His source was from another compartment which was totally out of Jim's control in the MCC (Missile Control Center.) On watch one night was a character by the name of Fred Scachiti. Fred played a tape of The Beatles with "Hey Jude" on it. J.P. called the MCC and requested that Fred play "Hey Jude" one more time if he could. Fred played "Hey Jude" over and over again for the entire watch period,

## First Patrol

driving Jim Riley nuts. He was determined to get even, but Fred Scachiti was a master at being a pain in the ass.

Meanwhile in the Wardroom, Dr. Ross, who had no military training, was upsetting the norms of behavior and protocol. Everyone was supposed to wait for the Captain to sit before doing the same. Dr. Ross, however, would just sit upon entering the Wardroom and then get nudged to stand up and wait. This happened time and time again, which Captain Ellis found very humorous. Dr. Ross also made his fellow officers grimace when he used copious quantities of ketchup on everything, including steak. And believe me, the food we had onboard was the best available, especially the aged beef we were issued. My mouth is watering right now just thinking about my many steak experiences onboard the five submarines on which I was privileged to serve.

Now back to Dr. Ross. Captain Ellis finally had a slight hissy fit when Dr. Ross covered his steak in ketchup. This was the last straw. Captain Ellis asked him politely to consider eating with the crew from then on. Without any hesitation, Dr. Ross joined our throng, and his eating habits blended in with ours. For the rest of the patrol, we had many a laugh at the expense of our new stepchild and provocateur.

At the start of every patrol, I started my own tradition. I shaved my head and stopped shaving my face. It amounted to less baggage—no shaving gear and no shampoo. At the end of each patrol, we would hold a best-beard contest. I will complete that story later.

The shrink, Dr. Wired or Dr. Weird, floated around the sub like a cloud, taking notes and observing. One day Dr. Weird found a quiet spot in between four missile tubes. There was only one way in, and he sat down to do some paperwork. When he tried to exit, he was confronted with J. P. Riley with his penis and scrotum exposed and the velcro closure/fly cinched up in such a way that everything protruded. Jim was dancing from one foot to the other with his cock and balls flapping all over the place. Dr. Weird abruptly turned to escape and spotted Joe Gemma (Sonarman) twenty feet away in a similar condition dancing from foot to foot. Jim and Joe were doing the *dick dance*. The poor shrink made it back to his stateroom and didn't venture out for a very long time. This was a one-time occurrence onboard any submarine. It can be described as an impromptu event purposely invented to shake this prude up.

On the other hand, Father Brown was a delight and was always available. He held great religious services; however, he didn't escape our need for humor, either. One day we snuck into his stateroom and got hold of his brand-new white sneakers and wrote all over them—right foot, left foot, port, starboard, six toes, five toes. He took it in stride and wore them for the whole patrol.

## A Major Tragedy Onboard

The Tech Reps were terrific guys. However, one of them showed signs of stress, although he was trying to hold his own. The daily routine was augmented and improved upon with a daily movie shown in the crew chow hall. These were sixteen-millimeter reels housed in rather large carrying cases and stored in the lower-level missile compartment. All seventy

## First Patrol

or eighty movie boxes remained there along with thirty crates of eggs. Yes, eggs—unrefrigerated, but in the cool lower level.

During my watch, my main task was to monitor all sixteen missile tubes and the missiles therein. We never revealed the true number of missiles we carried. That number was classified and on a "need to know basis." If any moisture accumulated in the eject chamber in the bottom of the missile tube, the watchstanders would notice immediately. The watchstanders sat in front of a long line of electronic panels to monitor them and be prepared to launch all missiles in a very short period of time, if necessary. I will tastefully leave this very sensitive topic and get on with less politically sensitive ones. However, one of my watch cycles was to become a life-altering experience.

I interrupt myself out of context to mention a special fellow submarine sailor. His name was Jimmy Augustus Snyder—slight of frame with premature hair thinning and maybe weighing in at one hundred forty pounds or thereabouts. Jimmy's responsibilities, his watch station, was in the Auxiliary Room #1, just beyond the missile compartment and just beyond a non-watertight bulkhead. His responsibilities included life-support apparatus—$CO_2$ scrubbers, oxygen generators, and some other vital pieces of equipment.

Jimmy was also qualified to run our movie projectors. As per U.S. Navy dictates, if a qualified movie operator was not available due to watch cycles, we looked for Jimmy. Even if he was in the kip in a deep sleep, without a word of complaint, Jimmy would head to the chow hall and make a whole bunch of submariners very happy to be able to watch a movie (and sometimes two) to escape the boredom and the monotonous routine. Jimmy was a caring, genuinely great guy, and a great sub mate.

Back to my watch from HELL. Halfway through my six hours of babysitting all potential sixteen missiles, a tremendous explosion occurred. It was mind-altering and large enough to shake dust and debris from the confusion of cables and piping in the overhead of the entire missile compartment. I instantly monitored all of my missiles and other associated ordnances and realized it had nothing to do with missiles in any way, which was a great relief to me. I also automatically draped a sound-powered communication headset on me to tap into the submarine emergency communication network. This was automatic procedure throughout the submarine. I then instructed my Roving Patrol to make a fact-finding sweep throughout the missile compartment. In the middle-level missile compartment were a number of bunks—fifteen in all. The explosion had everybody in those bunks up and about, getting oriented and quickly helping the Roving Patrol to pinpoint the origin.

The sub was then taken to periscope depth and the main ventilation system lined up to exchange all of the air in the sub—getting rid of any contaminated air onboard. It seemed that the exact location was pinpointed to Oxygen Generator #2. One of the other qualified watchstanders for this area put on air-breathing apparatus and, through all of the smoke and debris, he found his friend and fellow watchstander. You guessed it. Jimmy Augustus Snyder was lying on his back, unconscious and non-responsive. With the help of others who arrived on the scene, Jimmy was carried in stages from the

## First Patrol

Auxiliary Room #1 down through the port-side middle level of the missile compartment. Concurrently, fellow crewmembers were preparing the aft part of the crew's mess (chow hall) and transforming it into an operating room or surgical theater, as per design.

The ship's doctor, Dr. Ross, did all he could, but to no avail. While on the operating table, Jimmy bled out and died. The atmosphere—the movement and conversation—was restricted to official operational military/submarine efficient operations.

I, just now, took an unscheduled pause in my writing and my mind was overwhelmed with Jimmy's presence. I really believe that Jimmy was trying to make contact with me. He was thanking me for remembering him so kindly. He told me that all other mention of him was in morbid-incident reports, which never alluded to him as a person—a person with hopes and dreams and as a loving family man. In my mind, he finished by saying, "How about let's go to the chow hall—I'll break out the projector, and we will watch a flick and drink some coffee." I am crying right now, realizing that my disturbed sleep last night was all about Jimmy wanting me to get my ass up and out of bed, so that he could pay me a visit! My body is numb, and I have chills all over; this happens to me every time I reread this. My reference to Jimmy was going to be at an adequate level in my little book, but I now understood that, for fifty-seven years, Jimmy has been waiting for me to tell more of his story—even the last part which will really piss everyone off!

Back to the scene on the sub. Grown men, fearless submariners were looking like zombies with tears in their eyes. One of our Band of Brothers had fallen. One day Jimmy was just a guy from middle America who decided to serve his country, and through determination, he became a Nuclear-Powered Submariner. His task was to be part of a highly trained and dedicated group of men who would be on patrol and make the enemies of the United States acutely aware of our heavily armed submarines that could annihilate them. Our true purpose was *deterrence* defense, not offense. And that is what Jimmy ultimately gave his life for.

Jimmy's body was lovingly prepped and placed in a body bag. Just before departing from the tender as we stored all of our provisions, a box was delivered containing two body bags. We hadn't realized the significance or irony of that, because they were the first body bags ever issued to a sub, and we now needed to use one. The body bag containing Jimmy's remains was then placed into the walk-in freezer.

## Explosion

Back to the scene of the explosion once again—$O_2$ Generator #2. The generators onboard had blowout panels that were clad all around the entire unit. The purpose for this was for easy access, and if there ever was an explosion (worst-case scenario), the blast would dissipate out of many points of exit, not confining the blast. A major contained explosion could have far-reaching destructive consequences. It became the custom to leave the blow-out panels off, which was a widely accepted and sanctioned procedure throughout the fleet. It made for easy access for maintenance and unobstructed visual inspection.

## First Patrol

However, we had recently received a message directing all submarines to put all blow-out panels back on the generators from this point on.

The $O_2$ generator consists of distilled water supplied by our 5000-gallon-a-day still in the Engine Room. The generator then breaks the water down, and the one-part hydrogen and two-parts oxygen is split. The hydrogen is pumped and discharged out to sea through a hull penetration, while the remaining oxygen, in a gaseous form, is compressed into rather large oxygen bottles for dispersal upon needs onboard the sub.

So those blow-out panels had been installed for a couple of days. It was deduced that Jimmy had an alarm indicating a hydrogen leak was detected; however, when Jimmy went to the generator, the accumulation of the hydrogen was gross, and a spark from within the generator triggered a violent explosion. The recently installed blow-out panels blew out, and one hit Jimmy in the face, flipping him backwards; the back of his head hit a relief valve, crushing his skull. The compartment was full of smoke and debris. You know the rest of the story. What if the blow-out panels had not been in place? Would Jimmy have survived?

Eating onboard took a shift immediately. Nothing out of that freezer was consumed, and for the next five days many sandwiches were prepared from the contents of another freezer. Our CO broke radio silence, and five days later, we surfaced in a neutral non-patrol area, and a British helicopter rendezvoused with us. Jimmy's remains were solemnly carried through the sub for the last time and departed through a watertight topside hatch that was just above where he so faithfully stood his watches and the spot where he died. One crewmember by the name of Holland, who was a very close friend of Jimmy's, accompanied him. The helicopter hovered above the missile deck of the sub, and Jimmy's body was hoisted up to and into the helicopter. As the hoist line was lowered, Holland was hoisted up and climbed aboard the copter; with a gentle rise and acceleration, Jimmy was on his way home.

Many onboard suffered in their own unique ways. Some never watched another movie for the rest of the patrol, and quite a few refused to eat anything that came out of that freezer again. Jimmy's bunk area became a sort of shrine. A cross appeared on his pillow, along with a set of rosary beads, or a comb for the little hair he had on top of his head, or a stuffed teddy bear, which had been given to one of the crewmembers by his kids. Everyone wanted to share some love with Jimmy.

The rest of the patrol was solemn, and we all became a lot more introspective and more keenly aware of the danger we were living with on a constant basis. We further understood why we received a substantial hazardous-duty pay.

## *Story: Beard-Growing Contest*

Let's change course and get to a lighter side. As time went on, we tried to get back to a more relaxed state of mind, still respecting what had happened that resulted in an untimely death. Our patrol was coming to an end, and it was time to have a little fun by naming the winner of the beard-growing contest.

The Tech Rep (civilian) onboard possessed what could be considered a Hollywood makeup artist's dream beard,

## First Patrol

but he had to be removed from the contest. His nerves had become so rattled over the course of the patrol, especially because of the aforementioned incident onboard, that chunks of his hair and his beard started to fall out. With his elimination, and with all other contestants summarily pushed to the wayside, yours truly, Alan S. Votta, won the Best Beard Contest. The applause was deafening. My prize was a can of beer—a can of Coors beer, the beer the Captain confiscated the day of our departure after the beer had unexpectedly shown up on deck.

I could have sold that beer for $100 plus. I snatched my prize from the Captain himself, chilled it, and with the CO's permission, I sipped it like it was 100-year-old MacCallum Scotch whiskey. It was so good, and it was a moment I will never forget. I did give a sip or two to special friends, and we giggled like little kids over the scene of where we were and what a can of beer could do for one's morale. So, if you feel guilty about loving beer, tell the world to just "pound sand" and "kiss my ass!" BEER! Plenty good!

The Tech Rep, originally the one with the great beard, had to be escorted off the submarine once we were in port. I'll never forget his name—Gary Cundom. Yes, we played with his name, and he was called "Mr. Condom." We watched as Gary left the sub. Later we were told that Gary recovered from his frayed nerves; he contacted us to get the details of the terrible incident onboard, so that he could pay his last respects to Jimmy Snyder's wife. We all applauded him for that, and we gained a hearty respect for his initiative, as well as his ability to conquer his personal inner demons.

## Change-of-Command

It was the Blue Crew's turn to man the railings of the tender. They watched us (The Gold Crew) bring home their charge, which was to be their responsibility for the next refit, sea trials, and deterrent patrol. There were many who were glad to be back, but there were always a few who were not so happy to be back. I kept my distance from those sourpusses and put their feelings out of my mind.

Three days of change-of-command were filled with the visits of investigators from many governmental agencies, engineers, tech reps, and submarine military brass, in order to scrutinize everything surrounding the accident and Jimmy's death. They were very eager to examine and dissect the $O_2$ generator #2. The manufacturer of the generator was Treadwell Corporation, and they were under plenty of pressure to pinpoint the problem area, discover any other weak spots, and solve the problem, so as to never have that happen again. Remember, there were twenty to twenty-five subs with these $O_2$ generators on board. One order was sent to all subs. "Pronto! Remove explosion plates indefinitely."

Since it was change-of-command day, those of us from the Gold Crew were chomping at the bit, ready physically and mentally for some well-earned R&R. We were now finally out of our poopy suits (with the trap door), which were better known as nuclear submarine coveralls, and into our white dress uniforms. We had fully morphed into a sea of white—stampeding eager sailors wanting to get home as fast as possible. We boarded buses at the docks and were driven to the airbase

## First Patrol

a mile away. As we boarded our flights, we were divided into two planes once again—half of the crew on each.

It was great to see stewardesses. Did I date myself just then? Before being called *flight attendants*, the professional staff onboard airlines were called "stewardesses." They were extremely caring, and I might add, all were very easy on the eyes. As we were boarding, one of our crew members whispered loudly into the ear of the man in front of him, "Did you remember the bomb?" Now you have to remember that, during this time period, sky-jackings and bomb threats onboard airplanes was an all-too-frequent reality.

After sitting on the airplane for a while, it became apparent that there was a problem, and the plane was being delayed. We soon found out why. One of the stewardesses overheard the word *bomb*, and she discreetly notified her pilot. The pilot enacted proper procedure and notified the authorities. Soon we were visited by two gentlemen (honest to God) wearing trench coats and looking like two guys from a Tom Clancy spy novel/movie. They were directed to the idiot who spoke the foolish words. To set the record straight, this jerk-off who had uttered the dreaded word was the one total shithead in the crew—the one not caught in the rigorous sifting and filtering process to make sure that unsavory characters like him would not make it through to "crew quality status." This character somehow snuck through the system and he, consequently, was the one guy we all learned to avoid—even in the tight confines of the submarine—except on a professional basis. The other crewmember to whom the remark was directed simply smiled and told him to "Shut up." Even so, the fool and the innocent crewmember were directed by the two Naval Investigative Service Officers to follow them, and off the airplane they went.

We were stunned to realize that, after all preparations for takeoff had been finalized, we flew off, minus two crewmembers. Think about the family members who were expecting them back in Charleston and the wives who were going to be shocked and dismayed. It took a full week for the matter to be reconciled, and the aforementioned dickheaded perpetrator was never to ride a submarine again. Just desserts, if you ask me. The fool was delayed on purpose by the authorities for still another week while the innocent second party was released. He took an afternoon hop (flight) home to finally reunite with his family. We were told that the release sequence was purposely planned because the innocent victim was so upset with the perpetrator that the authorities feared that some severe retribution might occur. The victim, or better known as the innocent one, reunited with his family, and he mellowed quickly. He took the incident in stride and was welcomed back heartily.

His name was Abe Varner. Abe had a relative who was stationed at the Naval Air Base Rota—the very one that we flew in and out of. What made this extra special was that one of his relatives flew cargo flights to Incirlik, Turkey. He fulfilled orders for expensive items like watches, jewelry, and meerschaum pipes. Back in the day, these pipes were used by many sailors onboard subs. I bought five different pipes for under $30. Stateside, each pipe could easily cost $50 and up. So that was another reason that we welcomed back Abe. I could not master pipe smoking. It wasn't for me. So, a year later, I gave them all to my brother, who was quite excited to receive them. Yes, this sort of merchandise enterprise was somewhat shady and maybe illegal, but it kept the morale of many a sailor high.... despite the slight cut Abe's cousin took for his efforts.

## Story: Growing Pains

This has reminded me of something that I completely overlooked, which happened only a week into our patrol, and I must include this story before going any further. There were three Annapolis Midshipmen who were making the patrol with us. Instead of having the summer off, these midshipmen were dispatched on temporary orders to bases, ships, and subs, depending on their training path. Of the three, two were great and were eager to fit in and work their asses off. However, the third individual was, from the start, unbelievably arrogant and rude, and he exhibited a privileged attitude. His father was Admiral Black, and young Mr. Black thought he was heir apparent to his father's achievements and respect without having ten minutes of active duty under his belt. But he was in for a rude awakening. Everyone onboard tried to make life miserable for him on a daily basis.

One evening, as he was making his way back to the engineering spaces, he stopped in the Auxiliary Room #1. He stopped because he heard an alarm going off, which piqued his curiosity. By the way, this was the same compartment where Jimmy Snyder met his demise. He found the watchstander, who was merely testing a handheld freon detector and calibrating it for future routine usage. Wally Cox was the watchstander, and he instantly saw an opportunity. He put on a very serious face and told Midshipman Black that the device was a new type of Geiger counter, and apparently the alarm was sounding because there was nuclear contamination suddenly nearby. Wally told Black, whom we had nicknamed "Black Cloud," that the alarm occurred right around the time he'd entered the compartment.

Wally directed him to stand still; Wally pointed the working end of the freon detector at B.C. and purposely triggered the alarm. B.C. was directed to stand still and not to move. Wally made a couple of strategic phone calls, which resulted in me and a handful of other merrymakers to break out RADCON gear (Radiation Contamination gear.) We all scurried around B.C. and as each step was taken, his eyes grew larger and larger. We donned all of the appropriate yellow contamination coveralls, wore air-breathing masks, and covered the path to Auxiliary Machinery #2 with yellow plastic film right through the Reactor Compartment and up to the designated decontamination shower. We continuously monitored B.C. with the freon counter, with the alarm intermittingly going on and off to make it all seem as real as possible.

Finally, B.C. was at the shower, and he was instructed to strip down naked; his personal belongings were bagged up in a yellow bag marked *contaminated*. He was then instructed to get into the shower and wash away any surface contamination—with strictly cold water, because warm water would open his pores and allow the contamination to enter his sweat glands! Remember, we may have been somewhere in the North Atlantic (I cannot say for certain because of top secrecy); however, the water-injection temperature at that point was in the high 30-degree range, as it affected the potable water

## First Patrol

temperature onboard. Let's just say the shower temperature was unbelievably COLD. B.C. entered the shower (the valve controls, of necessity, were mounted *outside* the shower stall). Once he was in, the door was closed and held closed. As the water hit B.C.'s body, he tried to exit the shower, but the door was unyielding. After some pleas and begging from him, we opened the shower door to see the most pitiful sight revealed. However, he was not allowed to exit because when the freon detector was directed at him again—lo and behold, it went off again! Imagine that. The door was shut once more, and the water turned on. In an instant, we, the instigators, rushed to restore all gear and clear the area of all RADCON material; then we disappeared from sight. With the water turned off, B.C. exited the shower to find not another soul in sight; neither were any of the yellow contamination decorations in sight. And most important of all, his clothes were nowhere to be seen.

Slowly, but surely, B.C. started to put two and two together, but he was still confused. How was he going to get to his bunk, soaking wet, bare-ass naked, through five compartments? By this time the word, of course, had spread throughout the sub, and the path B.C. had to travel was filled with a gauntlet of gawkers and voyeurs. The Captain had tactfully stayed in the background, playing the *plausible deniability* card. The amazing outcome was that B.C. became a totally different person after that ordeal, and he became a pleasure to have around. It was an illustration, you might say, that a little tough love can have a resounding effect.

I was proud to see this transformation. The U.S. Navy benefited because Mr. Black eventually also achieved the rank of Admiral, and he became a terrific CO onboard two different submarines. He was a tough, well-liked, and respected submariner. And, I might add, he used this story and experience many times over to make a point to junior officers as he was climbing the ranks.

## Back in Charleston

Jumping ahead and back to arriving in Charleston after patrol, we entered the R&R period for approximately thirty days, and that flowed into a retraining period and refresher training. The Fleet Ballistic Missile Submarine Training Center had, as previously stated, an entire submarine installed in classrooms and oversized enclosed engineering spaces, all assembled in a rather large brick building instead of a metal hull. It also included a missile tube and a torpedo tube. The purpose of this was to keep our skills fresh and sharp because we eventually would be boarding planes back to Rota, Spain, and after another change-of-command, we would resume refitting and be back on patrol again.

The R&R came to an end, and our first full crew gathering, affectionately called 'mustering," was to occur. Through the grapevine, we heard that something of a very sensitive nature was going to be discussed. The next morning arrived, and there was some gossip about Jimmy Augustus Snyder floating around that we would not be happy about. We all finally assembled, and the Captain came to the point quickly. After a very professional greeting and welcome-back statement, he simply said that there had been a major fuck-up with the

## First Patrol

way Jimmy's loved ones were treated, but more importantly, prematurely told about his demise. It seems that in the chain of custody of his remains, the team that was being assembled to inform Jim's wife was circumvented by some lowlife fucker who took it upon himself to call Jim's wife and simply asked, "What do you want to do with your dead husband's remains?"

We all knew Jimmy's story and background. He and his wife had had a difficult time conceiving a child, and, after much fretting and anxiety, they had decided to adopt. The adoption had occurred just before our departure, and Jimmy and his wife were able to share only a few happy days before we all had to depart. So, with a new baby, Jim's wife was primping and preparing and eagerly awaiting her loving husband's return to her and their new baby. But instead—some coldhearted, uncaring individual decided to take it upon himself and circumvent the time-tested emotional-support protocol and utmost respectful conveyance of the tragic death of a military loved one. The entire crew was outraged, and many of us wanted to find that son-of-a-bitch and do him in. The crew was so agitated that all of our ranks were broken, and many had tears in their eyes.

However, the most upset and angered person was our Captain. He helped us to calm down a little as he let go with an immense tirade of disgust. By then we all had to try to console him, but we also wanted to know what would happen to punish this thoughtless soul. Captain Ellis asked us all to coordinate and help Mrs. Snyder in any way possible. Without her husband, her life took an entirely new path, which included a move back to Pennsylvania to be close to her family and to Jim's family. Wives of our crewmembers took over (Casualty Assistance Centers), and her every need was fulfilled. All chores around her home were covered until she moved, and Jim's remains were respectfully handled all the way to Pennsylvania.

The point is that, we, as a crew, performed the maximum effort to make a terrible situation bearable without being overpowering, confusing, and unmanageable. And we were proud of what we tried to do for her. However, there was another ramification of that whole ordeal. Time marched on. In Naval lore, the Captain of a ship or sub is ultimately the person held responsible for all the glory or all of the blame. It seems that Captain Ellis's path to promotion took a mighty big hit because of someone dying onboard his command. In a short period of time, he was forced to retire prematurely. This is how the Navy works, unfortunately. He was a damn good CO and one hell of a person. "Fair Winds and Smooth Sailing."

The next couple of patrol cycles were, luckily, uneventful. Many additional stories accumulated during that time that will be told in another volume—if there is any acceptance of this, my Shakespearean debut, and if my editor (my wife) throws big bucks at me and begs me to write a sequel. I can dream, can't I? However, there are still two stories that I want to tell here.

## Story: Italian Fisherman

This story is from one of our subsequent patrols in the middle of the Mediterranean Sea. Our patrol area kept us in deep

## First Patrol

water near the Straits of Sicily. In our operating status, we would come to periscope depth to receive what we called a *blast* from a satellite—a message sent and received in mere seconds, consisting of many lines of data and code, which to some degree is still considered sensitive and classified top secret. We reached periscope depth after our sonar capability gave us a tentative "all clear."

At scope depth, the Officer of the Deck would latch on to the scope (#1 periscope), raise the scope, and start spinning around to scan the horizon. Because of temperature layers and density of salt in the water, a visual check was the only surefire way of telling whether there was any surface vessel nearby and a threat to us for a possible collision. That would not have been acceptable.

At this point, I have to back up a little and give some background for what is to come. As the nuclear submarine program was growing rapidly, it became a real problem to find potential submariners because of the strict and rigorous requirements placed on all possible volunteers. One particular and specific stipulation was that officers could not be considered if they had to wear glasses. You will see why shortly! However, the Navy had reached a point when they dropped the 20/20 eyesight rule and allowed officers wearing glasses, in order to include an additional pool of officers who were needed to man the new submarines that were being built.

Now back to the boat. When we reached periscope depth, the Officer of the Deck (an officer wearing eyeglasses) latched on to #1 periscope and started to spin around, as the working end of the scope broke through the surface. As he spun around, somehow the O.D. (Officer of the Deck) managed to knock his glasses off, and they fell down into the periscope storage well. He was unable to do his job. He was paralyzed and of no use. In an instant, for the safety of the sub, a quick judgment was made. The Quartermaster of the Watch took over the Diving Officer's position, and the Diving Officer took over my post (Chief of the Watch), which freed me to jump up onto the periscope stand and take over the Officer of the Deck position.

    I grabbed the periscope and immediately started spinning the scope around in a quick 360-degree rotation to check for any surface craft in the area that might do us harm. Meanwhile the O.D I had relieved was tucked away in a secure spot to keep him safe. Relieved that no imminent danger was present, I called out "No visual contacts. All clear." However, I did see something that motivated me to make another pass around to clarify and analyze. As I came around slightly forward and to starboard, I focused on an Italian fisherman in his little boat, smoking a pipe, who was staring intently at my scope and lens with a look of total amazement and disbelief. I could only imagine what was going on in his mind. He remained transfixed on the scope head, and we gently glided by as I turned the scope to let him know that something or someone was focused on him. At that time, we had a camera capability still attached to the scope, and, in an instant, I took many shots of the old fisherman as we were gliding by on nuclear power—what a contrast, to say the least!

    Another Qualified Officer of the Deck then came to the periscope stand. I made my report to him, and I relinquished

## First Patrol

my temporary post, stating aloud (as is the custom), "I have turned over the Deck to Mr. Nicholson." After the shuffle of posts, I was back to the Chief of the Watch post, and the Dive Officer went back to the Dive position between the planesman and the Quartermaster at the Navigation Station.

Ultimately, after the appropriate review of the incident, one solution was implemented quickly. The bespectacled Officer of the Deck had to secure his glasses by means of elastic material to his head. Additionally, he was always accompanied by another non-glasses-wearing Officer of the Deck when he was on duty and a periscope-depth maneuver was to occur. Luckily, we did not go to periscope depth very often. His career was salvaged, and a fleet-wide order was generated that all officers onboard would have elastic restraining straps attached to glasses to prevent another recurrence of what happened onboard the *USS Nathan Hale*.

The Italian-fisherman experience prompted me to request a copy or two of the pictures I took through the scope. In turn, I was promptly reminded that these shots were classified as *top secret* and could only be downgraded after eight years—I would have to wait that long before I would have any chance of securing any copies. The patrol continued, and there were no more incidents. Fast forward a few years from this patrol, and I was flipping through a copy of *Naval Proceedings*, a wonderful magazine available to the Naval-officer world. Whenever I had the opportunity to latch onto a copy, I read it from cover to cover, loving the great historical stories and current-affairs articles.

Approximately two or maybe three years had gone by since our Sicilian Straits experience, and I had a copy of *Naval*

*Proceedings* in my hand. What to my wonder, I fixated on two or three pages devoted to my Italian-fisherman photographs! I immediately questioned what had happened to the eight-year downgrading period. And the worst part of it all was that I was given no credit whatsoever, and the shots were erroneously credited to another submarine entirely. I got over my disappointment quickly, since I then had the pictures that I thought would never have been available to me. And don't I wish I knew where I put them for safekeeping! Incidentally, at present, I am pursuing those photos once again. In my ongoing research, I have discovered that it is possible to get copies of *Naval Proceedings* through the Naval Institute. Hopefully, they will appear again.

---

## Story: Throw Rug

I've got a story from one of my patrols that you may find hard to believe. Once again… this ain't no bullshit and may be as far-fetched a story as you'll ever hear. On one patrol a crewmember by the name of Alan Aldridge, who was a missile tech and an Old Salt and a real character, started a push to collect belly-button lint from all of the crewmembers. This strange and seemingly outlandish mission somehow caught on like wildfire, and, by the end of the patrol, there were many emptied cashew-nut cans full of lint. These cans became such treasured items that they were packed in top-secret shipping containers, so that customs could not inspect them when we

## First Patrol

flew home for R&R. The collected belly-button lint had made it unscathed to our home shore, much to the delight of all who participated.

Our first muster after the thirty-day R&R period ended was a rather different one, because several of the crewmembers' wives were present. This was highly unusual. After our CO finished with the business of the day, he introduced the wives present and stated that they had a gift to bestow on us. We unwrapped what looked like a rug about the size of a hand towel. We were essentially being presented with a small rug made from…. yes, you guessed it…. our belly-button lint. Alan Aldridge's wife, Dorothy, was the leader of the pack, and she, along with two other wives, combed the lint from the cans into yarn, and then wove it into the rug. Would you believe it? Yes, all the yarn was washed and sanitized.

We laughed like hell. This little event actually boosted our morale immensely. A month later, at our annual submarine crew party, an auction was held, and the rug was auctioned off. The winning bid was $325 and made by none other than the Chief of the Boat, Master Chief Tomosso—the top enlisted man onboard the sub. It became a prize possession of his, and he held on to that symbol of his crew for many years.

---

I really could go on forever telling story after story from my patrol days, but I did want to get these last two in because they were so unique.

# D. OTHER SUBS AND COMMANDS

To put my career into perspective, I should make you aware of the length and breadth of my wonderful and varied submarine experience. Not only was I involved with the building of the *Nathan Hale* from start to commissioning and subsequent patrols, I also was fortunate enough to do the same on the *USSBN George Marshall* 654 and its patrols thereafter. That was followed by renovating the *USS Entemador* SS 340, a World War II-vintage diesel submarine. After that I was stationed at the Navy Base at Mer Island, California, to renovate/overhaul the *USS John C. Calhoun* 630 to upgrade its Polaris A-2 missile-launch system to accommodate the Polaris A-3 system.

All of this time and these experiences enabled me to travel far and wide and to see so many exotic wonders of this world. I served on several other submarines after I became a Naval

*Real Stories from a Nuclear Submariner*

instructor, which you will read about in the next section. [See page 201 for the Timeline of My Naval Career.]

*Alan Votta as RPOC from company yearbook, 1962.*

*Leading Company 101 at graduation ceremony displaying flags won. 1962.*

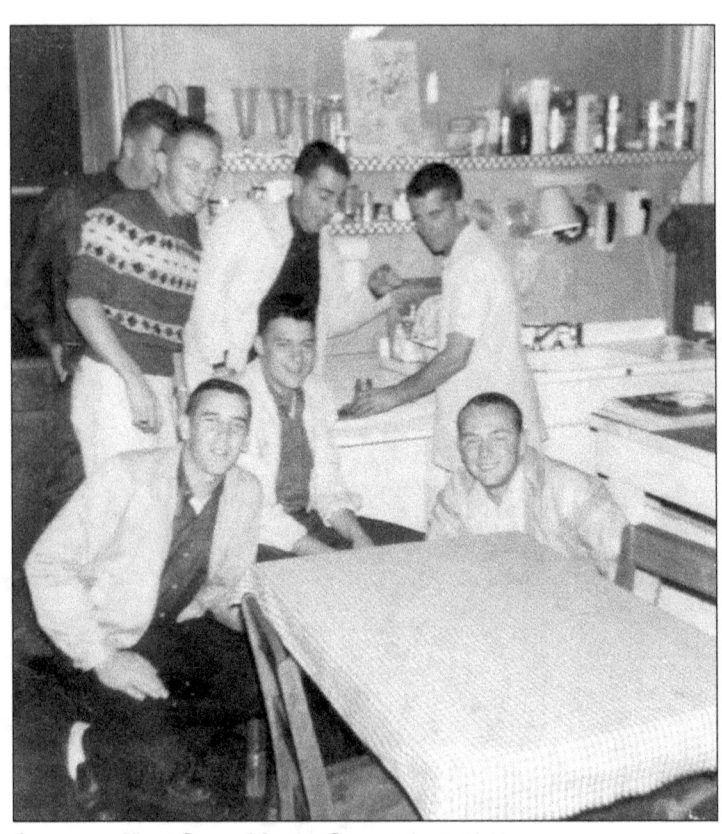

*Scavenger Hunt Story, Mystic, Connecticut, 1963.*

Torpedo Room onboard USS Nathan Hale, 1964.

Mess cooking in the Navy, 1964.

*Swim Call Mid-Atlantic off the George C. Marshall, 1966.*

*The USS George C. Marshall at sea, 1968.*

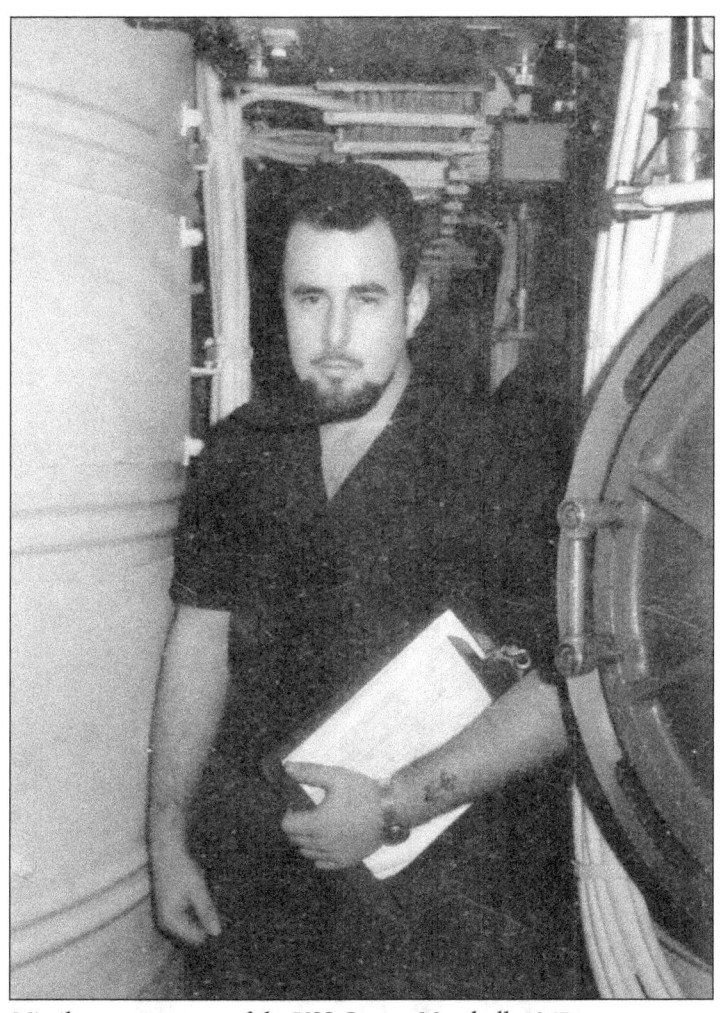

*Missile compartment of the USS George Marshall, 1967.*

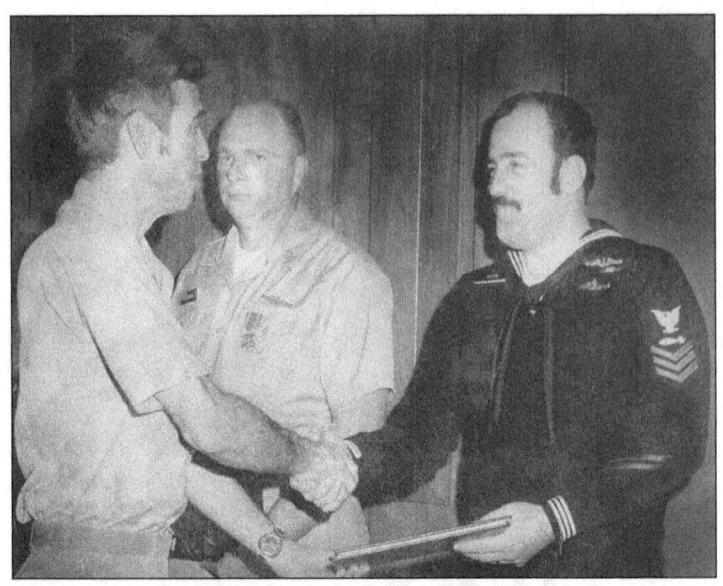

*Receiving merit award for nuclear weapons training, 1968.*

*Outstanding instructor awards, 1971.*

*Presented with Navy Achievement Award, 1972.*

*Instructors at Fleet Ballistic Missile Submarine Training Center, 1981.*

*Retirement Ceremony, 1983.*

*Memorabilia*

# Part Four

# Phase Two of My Naval Career

# A. Becoming a Naval Instructor

## 1. Naval Instructor Training School, Norfolk, Virginia

After a long period of deployments and patrols at sea, all of us onboard were then scheduled for what was called shore duty, i.e., no flights or refits and, thank God, no deterrent patrols. Because of my level of achievements and clean record, I was recruited to become a candidate for Naval Instructor Training School. This was quite an honor and a position of high esteem and recognition. Now detached from the *USS John C. Calhoun*, I traveled to the school's campus in Norfolk, Virginia. I was about to start the hardest and most challenging period of my life.

The Navy does not waste time. Their curriculum is results-proven and fair, but it is brutal. In a no-nonsense format, they toss information at you, and, if you don't catch on quickly, you are shown the front door. If you didn't make the grade, you would be politely eased out of the curriculum and recommended for a less-taxing shore assignment. Get the idea? Get up to speed quickly, or else!

Our introduction was frightening, and what we had to achieve was daunting. Each and every one of us—approximately forty students—had to create a course of instruction of our own choosing, from scratch, in a specific format and in time-specific segments. My head was reeling. Before the first day was over, three guys left before lunch break, and, at the end of the day, three more departed.

Detailed training on how to execute these desired results was presented to us, and we had to keep copious notes. There were no computers or electronic devices at all. They hadn't been invented yet! And everything was handwritten. The end product had to be duplicated and written out all over again, so that the instructor would have a copy to follow our presentation. All documents were written in pencil, including the finished lesson plan. There were times when I had so many erasures on my papers that I had to get a foxtail (handheld brush) to literally sweep away the eraser debris.

After finishing writing the lesson plan, we took our plan to the head (the men's bathroom) to practice our presentation in front of the many mirrors there. A timer (a stopwatch clock) was issued to each student, so that we could practice in a time-sensitive manner. Imagine four or five students in the men's room jabbering away on totally different topics and in different speaking styles. It was mayhem in the men's room. But it didn't matter, because everyone was so focused on what they were doing that the other students' chatter was no problem at all.

## Phase Two of My Naval Career

Each day, one, two, or three more students would depart. I have to mention that among us were about five civilians from different American corporations. The Naval Instructor Training Course was so highly regarded that these corporations paid big bucks to achieve entry. Two of the five had to depart because they couldn't keep up.

Finally, after the grueling days of instruction and practice, it was time to hand the main instructor our lesson plan, along with his copy, for it to be carefully scrutinized by the instructor. And you'd better believe that the structure—margins, headings, and legibility—had to be spot on. The instructor then handed us back our copy, and in front of our fellow students, we made our first presentation. This was just the warm-up for much more training. Our final presentation was a make-or-break circumstance of untold magnitude and proportion.

Our fellow students became our students. In an exact fashion, we had to check the identity of each student and verify that they belonged in the course—also in a specific and timely manner. Additionally, we had to check the comfort level of all participants, e.g., room temperature and lighting, etc. And, oh, yes, the instructor might sometimes sabotage the classroom environment, thus, we had to be leery of every single detail, as mundane as some aspects seemed to be. In this atmosphere, you might be faced with a student instructed to be a little disruptive on purpose, to throw you off your game. We presented our lesson plan in the best tradition of the Naval Instructor Creed to optimize the learning experience for all of our future-student needs. We were preparing submariners for their role onboard any and all submarines that they would ever serve on.

As I mentioned, this was the toughest and most difficult challenge of my lifetime. We started with forty excited and stimulated men, believing we could make the grade, only to be shaken to our core—only to realize that so many would not make it to become a United States Naval Instructor.

I never left the barracks or the classroom. I studied, wrote, and practiced for hours every day. When the final presentation for graduation arrived, I felt like I was as prepared as I could ever be. When that fateful day came, I passed my final presentation with flying colors—and I could finally breathe again. I really felt like I'd just graduated from Navy SEAL School! With a swagger in my step, I was presented with my instructor credentials. I was very proud and full of a sense of accomplishment.

## Story: A Dramatic Presentation

I have to reflect back and mention something, or someone, and his rather dramatic presentation—his final lesson plan. Of course, we were the audience/student body for one another's moment in the sun. Among the contestants was a Navy Corpsman by the name of Kowalski. We called him Doctor Kildare (another dating-me moment.) Doc was streaking along, and his lesson plan was about advanced first aid—way beyond iodine and a Bandaid. He was speaking in a fine, professional, and confident manner. He had us all enrapt in his subject matter. All of a sudden, he became tense, and he started to show signs of some unknown ailment, which seemed to come from nowhere. Doc grabbed his chest and let out a groan as he crumpled to the deck (floor). We all were in total

## Phase Two of My Naval Career

shock—especially the instructors. After a pregnant pause, with our hearts in our throats, suddenly Doc miraculously jumped to his feet.

We were all shocked beyond belief. Doc looked at everyone and simply said, "When I finish my lesson plan today, you will know exactly what to do, if, in the future, someone collapses in your presence." He won the Oscar! And he won the respect of the instructors and all of his fellow future instructors. He was given a special award—not quite a gold statue, but a certificate of special achievement and unique presentation.

---

In all, it took three to four days to allow the necessary time for our whittled-down crew, which now consisted of only nineteen of us, to finish our presentations. The best part was that the Last of the Mohicans all passed easily. It is difficult for me to leave this part of my book because it was the hardest, most grueling thing I had ever been part of or exposed to. It made all of the other achievements I had realized seem so minor.

I was now a United States Naval INSTRUCTOR. I was special, and I would soon face many classrooms filled with our Navy's finest. I would be shaping them into capable individuals to operate onboard nuclear submarines in a professional and prepared manner. I could even handle heart attacks! Thanks, Dr. Kildare.

Leaving Norfolk was a relief and an anxiously awaited event. It seemed that Norfolk, Virginia, was not so enamored with the vast Naval presence in their midst. Their dislike was so prominent that many businesses exhibited a pure love/hate approach. Many displayed very visual and conspicuous signs saying, "No Dogs or Sailors Allowed!" The Naval Command S.O.P.A. (Senior Officer Present Afloat) kind of ignored this treatment, thinking that it would all go away. But it got even worse. So S.O.P.A. released a base-wide order to boycott all businesses in Norfolk. The impact on the local economy was staggering. Remember that the base at Norfolk was composed of many diverse commands, and, in its total landmass, it was as big as the state of Rhode Island. In record time, the Norfuckians realized how much all of their economy depended on the sailors, whom they foolishly decided to hate, and who pumped millions of dollars into their pockets and their livelihoods. Let the healing process begin. Sailors were then looked upon quite differently—loved and respected once again.

## 2. Back to Charleston, South Carolina, and FBMSTC

After all graduation ceremonies concluded, with my orders in hand, I was on my way back to Charleston, South Carolina. I was to report directly to my new duty station at the Fleet Ballistic Missile Submarine Training Center.

After a little R&R, I proceeded to my new command and to a very special greeting prepared for me, as it was for all new instructors coming onboard. We were made to feel at home, and a senior instructor from the center conducted a one-on-one orientation. Throughout the building, I bumped into many old

## Phase Two of My Naval Career

acquaintances and familiar faces. Before the morning was out, I finally was assigned my area of instruction and met with all of my fellow instructors. There were warm and cordial greetings, including some sarcastic words like, "Where the fuck have you been?" and, "You took your sweet-ass time getting here," etc. I had not been on any sub with these gentlemen, so it was a new beginning, like having to work your way into a new family. It wasn't hard, because these guys were all so comfortable with who they were, and they were, through process of elimination, the finest and most sound-minded men alive. Considering those accolades, there was a vast difference of personalities, which was manifested in our combined sense of humor and made for some lively interaction.

Practical jokes were at the top of the list. For example, on my first full day on the job, one of my fellow instructors had to beg his peers to stop signing him up for magazine subscriptions. It seems he was suddenly receiving ten or fifteen magazines on a regular basis. He knew he had been had. Another instructor ordered a yard of sand and had it delivered and dumped on a fellow instructor's driveway. And the list went on. Winds up that, although these characters were a cut above, they were full of mischief. Over the next couple of years, we shared many fun moments, with lots of smiles and laughs along the way.

My assignment and teaching responsibilities were in the areas of Polaris missile tubes and launch panels and equipment. In addition, I was tasked with covering torpedo-tube training and torpedo loading and monitoring. I took on all of the challenges with pride and zeal. A few months later, I was informed that, due to my exemplary Naval performance, I was to be presented with the United States Naval Achievement Medal.

This was quite an honor. And to have it presented by Captain Samuel Ellis, who happened to be available, made it super special for me. Commander Ellis made an extraordinary effort to make my day distinctive, even though he was going through a personally trying period, and his retirement was imminent. After Jimmy's death, he was put in the hot seat, but he still had a positive attitude. The medal ceremony became a momentous occasion for me. I was specifically honored for my leadership and guidance in keeping our submarine launch capability at 100% during four patrols on the *USS George Marshall*. The medal was presented to me in an auditorium filled with my peers and family. I couldn't have been prouder.

## Story: More Color in and Around the FBMSTC

The trials and tribulations of being a Naval Instructor could be a book of its own. However, there were a couple of memorable moments I'd like to retell here. For instance, one day I was on the second deck of FBMSTC in the close proximity of the auditorium where the Navy Achievement Award had been presented to me, where a Commanding Officer Change-of-Command ceremony was to take place. Many dignitaries, both civilian and military, were headed in the direction of the auditorium. I spotted one three-striper and his entourage coming up in the rear. He was obviously one of the COs who was either coming or going—the new or the old. As the group drew closer, I noticed something odd. As the CO came closer

## Phase Two of My Naval Career

to me, I instinctively put my hand out and stopped him in his tracks—my hand on his chest.

Needless to say, his reaction was one of total shock, and he started demanding an explanation. All I could do was make a hand gesture. I pointed at his chest and his many medals and insignias—quite impressive, but….. they'd been placed on the wrong side of his uniform! When he finally became aware of the error, his demeanor toward me changed dramatically from "Kill!" to "Hug!" He asked me where he could find the nearest head, and he asked me to follow him. Our combined efforts corrected what could have been a very embarrassing change-of-command. It would not have been a good look for the new CO to take over a brand-new command with such a glaring mistake obvious to all. Think of the comments and clichés that might ensue. "Starting off on the wrong foot!" Jokes would follow him forever.

His name was Commander Demins. He told me that his wife had wanted to help prepare him for the ceremony. She did a great job, but she got it just a little bit wrong. In record time, because of our combined efforts, the uniform FUBAR was rectified. With a hearty handshake and a face-saving hug, Commander Demins' Change-of-Command was a resounding success, instead of being a disaster of unknown proportions. I wound up with a friend for life. He was a commander with an exceptional personality and military bearing—a true cut above.

## Story: New Chief

Within our instructor ranks, new personnel were always coming and going. One day we were notified that our launcher, missile, and fire-control areas would have a new senior enlisted leader. His name was Master Chief Trumbull, and he was an old, crusty, cantankerous *salty character*. He had the demeanor of a drill sergeant in need of a painful root canal. However, I thought I saw a chink in his armor. I detected an old softy in wolf's clothing. A short time elapsed before Chief Trumbull was to be formally sworn in. During that time, I further solidified my judgment about him; but I was the only one who thought that way. Everyone else was already trembling in fear of the day that Chief Trumbull would formally take over. The ceremony was conducted at a full instructor inspection in full dress uniform.

 The troops were all aligned on the drill field—awaiting the end of the short delay before the ceremony began. Therefore, our ranks were able to smoke and joke for a bit. I was inspired to leave my position and, in front of God and everybody, I proceeded to the front of the ranks and approached Chief Trumbull, who was being his typical grumpy self. The entire assembled group of instructors focused on my very suspicious movement toward Trumbull. You could have heard a pin drop. I looked at Chief Trumbull, and, in a voice loud enough for everyone to hear, I told him, "In boot camp we were told that, in the fleet, no matter what command was present, there would always be a Captain in charge with an executive officer to aid him in their mission. Furthermore, the Captain took

## Phase Two of My Naval Career

on the role of a *father*, and the Exec would be the *mother*." I continued on, telling him that our Captain was indeed a good father-like figure, but his exec was not a good mother figure. Consequently, we were adopting him—Chief Trumbull—as our new *mother figure!*

The reaction by the crowd was complete fear for me. To make things even more tenuous, I brazenly put my head on the chief's right shoulder. To everyone's astonishment—including mine—Chief Trumbull burst out in uncontrollable laughter. I was tremendously relieved.

The Chief was an avid pipe smoker, and, when he started to laugh, he blew air through his pipe, and burning embers from the pipe flew, with a number of embers landing on his obviously brand-new uniform. Each hot ember burned a little hole, which ruined his shirt and pants. At that moment, I felt the scene had taken a drastic new turn, and I was waiting for all hell to break loose—and not in my favor. But to my surprise, Chief Trumbull laughed even louder.... burned uniform and all.

And from that day on, the chief's nickname became *Mother*. He ate it up and wound up being one of the best Master Chiefs I ever had to work under. He and I had a very special relationship, marked by good, deep, profound discussions on student progress and achievement. But best of all were the belly laughs that we had together and as a group of dedicated instructors, which only enhanced our mission, objectives, and purpose. And he loved being called "Mother"—the moniker he carried proudly throughout the rest of his Naval career.

## Story: In the Classroom

To set the mood in my classrooms, I would start by having all students introduce themselves by indicating their name, hometown, and anything else they might want to share. This was a technique that would relax the atmosphere and hopefully make everyone feel comfortable. Following that introduction, I needed to verify each man's top-secret clearances by looking at every man's military ID card and comparing it against a list that would clear them for the course—or as we would say—*need to know*.

These were young guys, and the ID cards were the original cards issued in boot camp, when their hair was cut down to a five-o'clock-shadow level. The pictures on the IDs consequently were not too complimentary, as they had been snapped during a period of time when they all felt intimidated and somewhat scared. As I looked at ID after ID, I would make a remark and squeeze out a laugh about how terrible the picture was. In a short period of time, I got everyone looking at each other's ID, and, after much good, heartfelt laughter, my class mood was set.

The entire group became comfortable with one another. Friendships formed, the learning atmosphere was heightened, and security clearances were verified. All reports indicated that my classrooms were always a delight to be in. I was proud to know that my efforts as an instructor better prepared my students for our/their mission and for the objectives of the United States Nuclear Submarine Force.

## Phase Two of My Naval Career

I simply loved being an instructor, and I loved my time spent in Charleston as well as the whole atmosphere around the training center. Charleston was so rustic at that time, and venturing out off the base was always an experience. Back in the day, "All You Can Eat Buffets" were not very prevalent, and when one opened up in the area, many of us piled into multiple cars to give it a try. Truth to tell, as each one of these buffets opened, in a relatively short period of time, they failed. They underestimated the appetites of the United States Navy!

However, there were certain restaurants that could cater to the hordes of servicemen. They were the barbecue and fish fry joints that had been operating successfully since before the Civil War. Each had its own personality. The facilities were basic and earthy. Seating was on picnic benches with paper plates, plastic utensils, and fifty-five-gallon open-top drums as garbage receptacles. At one joint that my friends and I frequented, we watched in amazement as the family members of the barbecue restaurant hooked up a couple of garden hoses and washed down the entire interior of the restaurant, including counters, walls, and the picnic tables. Water came gushing out of the front door as we drove away, and we chuckled at this spectacle, which reminded me of an old western cowboy movie. It's just another example of what I witnessed in what, to my mind, was a rather backward, but wonderfully rustic way of life in this southern town.

# B. Real Life as a Submariner

## 1. Personal Life

It is time to bring in some of my personal life during all of this. I did have a personal life—but, honestly, it wasn't that pretty. I survived two dreadful marriages with two women I am not proud to say I called my wife. I will not go into a great deal of detail here, but suffice to say, my first marriage was reduced to a disaster, and my second, although it lasted much longer, was even worse. I wound up divorced from my first wife with the custody of three precious children. This marriage would take another book to explain correctly, and this is not the time to try to analyze it. I will say, however, that patrol separations did not help.

After my divorce from my first wife, it was a trying time to be a single dad, but the kids and I handled it well, and we survived. After being on my own for a few years and trying to make things work for us, I met a woman through the organization Parents Without Partners. After a proper courting period, we decided to marry. We combined families, and a thirty-year marriage was the outcome. The entire marriage was fraught with tension and many altercations. We tried marriage counseling by an esteemed psychologist. After many sessions with him, the good doctor wanted to see me one-on-one; he told me that my wife was a borderline paranoid schizophrenic, and he told me that she had refused treatment. In an exasperated tone, he simply looked at me and said, "She is fucked up," and he wondered how I'd lived with her so long. I was stunned. To hear such crude language from a respected professional was not what I expected. My only answer to him was that, on a daily basis, I tried to do something special to make the day better for her, thinking that would make her happy. I thought that good deeds could be the obvious cure, but I did not know how psychotic behavior and thinking could twist things. I know now how very wrong I was.

Time went by, and my wife became ill and rather secretive. As she got sicker and her illness progressed, I stood the watch and cared for her till the end.

Her passing became another adjustment for me. Truth be told, I had been planning to leave her and end the tumultuous marriage. Because she was suffering with so much illness, I chivalrously stayed by her side for many more years than I had wished. With my due diligence and obligation, I made her life as comfortable as possible. After her death, I was like a zombie—realizing that I was out from under the terrible grips of a tyrant.

So, that, in a nutshell, is the story of my two failed marriages.

## 2. A Major Decision

Before I explain how I made another major decision, I need to bounce back a bit. I was brief when I mentioned my first wife.

After we met and started dating, our relationship developed, and I felt good about things. All indications were that she seemed to be pretty squared away. There was so much I didn't know! Nevertheless, it looked good from all angles—until it was too late!

She was an enigma. After living together for a time, we eventually got married. And for the next eight years, I was stuck in a marriage that was a catastrophe. I was making patrols, and I had a wife who had the morals of an alley cat, as it soon became clear to me. More of her past rose to the surface, and it seemed like a seedy Hollywood B movie, starring Gullible Alan and co-starring his unscrupulous wife.

Eight years later, after I'd tried to make our marriage work, she abruptly moved out of our home. Oh, and by the way, we had three children by then (two of them fathered by me). But she did not want anything to do with them any longer and especially did not want anything to do with me. I ultimately felt relieved. The children wanted to be with me, and thus, our great experiment was about to begin. The single-dad world was a challenge.

One year later, our divorce was final, and I received sole custody of the children. One of our three children was a child she had by her ex-husband. Yes, the saga is much more involved and complicated. There are not enough words in *Webster's*

*Dictionary* to explain it all. After the divorce, she suggested that I adopt her son, who I was raising and loved as my own. She exited our home, and we never heard from her again. Let it be known, however, that there are a lot of details that I could fill another book with—just too complicating and confusing to cover now.

Let's get back to the Navy. Do you see a trend here? My home life—marriage #1 and marriage #2 were failures, but my Naval life was full of accomplishments. My life was a kind of two-sided scenario in some respects. I was managing, and the children were doing well. Their school work was all positive, and their general outlook on life improved, albeit without a challenging, unstable mother being around. Challenging times, however, lay ahead. My tour of duty at the Training Center would eventually be over, and submarine patrols would be the normal rotation.

I approached our new CO at the Training Center, believing that the submarine Navy always took good care of our men. I soon found out that the position of CO of the Training Center is the bottom of the totem pole of prestigious submariner duty assignments. The Pentagon was the top in prestige, as were other various choice assignments. Once meeting him, you knew that this CO was at the end of his Naval career, with no promotions in rank on the horizon. He had a chip on his shoulder and a rather negative attitude about most things. Instead of a positive meeting, a true disaster was brewing. His only startling recommendation to me was that I should put my children into an orphanage, so that the Navy could

## Phase Two of My Naval Career

recoup some of the money they'd spent on me for my extensive schooling and training!

This guy was a fellow submariner, a fellow Italian, and a fellow father of three children. The die was cast, and it looked like I would be leaving the submarine force. Now hear this, my friends. After that woeful meeting with the CO, I attempted to talk to a senior chaplain. It became apparent to me that this fellow, instead of being involved with his ministerial charges and duties, was more enamored with simply wearing a wonderful attention-getting uniform. This character cut our discussion short and would not make any positive gestures or moves to support my need to stay ashore and not go back to sea. He was more interested in going off to the Officers' Club for an afternoon of good food and drink and to rub elbows with the top brass in order to boost his own ego. He liked to play dress-up.

What I was attempting to do was buy some time and settle my predicament, so that I could make sure my children were properly cared for. Since the powers-that-be seemed not to care (at least the power brokers that I was forced to deal with), I formulated a plan of notifying various civilian contractors that I might be available. Within a week or less, I was being contacted by G.E., Westinghouse, Lockheed, and VITRO Laboratories. Out of the group seeking my employ, VITRO Labs had the best offer, with no extensive tech-rep travel requirements. The majority of the other offers would have required numerous trips to where the submarines were located—places like Guam, Hawaii, Holy Loch, Scotland, etc.

At VITRO my children and I would have stability and no separation. I accepted the VITRO offer.

My enlistment was about up, and there we were, the four of us, now released by the Navy and closing out unfinished business in Charleston, South Carolina. Our household goods were packed up, and a moving van was headed to Silver Spring, Maryland. Thus started our grand adventure. All of us were crammed into a 1962 Volkswagen Bug. (I had given my ex-wife the family car because she could not drive a stick shift.) It was all fine with me—as long as the kids and I were happy.

The trip was a great experience, taking us three days to get there. We stopped at every scenic and historical attraction along the way. After finally arriving in Maryland, the task at hand was finding a home. We fell in love with Columbia, Maryland, an entire new town complete with shopping mall, theater, parks, and petting zoo. Most important of all was that the school the kids would be attending was within walking distance of home….very protected with walking paths and foot bridges. They never had to encounter an active roadway or crosswalk. We found a beautiful secluded townhouse in Hannibal Grove. This decision was cozy, warm, and delightful, and the four of us agreed that it was terrific. We settled in and instantly started to love our new life and surroundings.

Assuming the title of Staff Engineer, I checked in with my new employer. I was impressed at once with my choice of VITRO. The welcoming ceremony was great, and the challenging work to follow was exciting and engaging—Top Secret—stuff I still cannot talk about.

## Phase Two of My Naval Career

We took one day at a time, and my little family and I settled happily in. Our together time was marked by visiting every tourist attraction in the nearby DC area. We spent an inordinate amount of time at the Smithsonian. At this point in time, Charles Lindbergh's plane, the *Spirit of St. Louis,* was hanging from the overhead at the entrance to one of the main buildings. I jumped up and touched the starboard tire and picked up each of my children so they could touch this marvelous piece of history. I was glad that I did that because eventually, the Space Museum was built, and, although the *Spirit of St. Louis* remained on display, it was untouchable and inaccessible. My crew and I got to know DC quite well, and a love affair was generated for great American history. Our touring included the battlefields at Gettysburg—a palpable experience, which to my mind should be on everyone's bucket list.

### *Story: Back Home and Back to Work*

I was well into the routine at VITRO, and I soon realized that day-to-day within the organization was like being in the Navy (without having to wear a uniform), because of the number of ex-submariners on staff. If you needed a haircut, you just told your boss, and off you went; if you needed to renew your license or take care of other personal needs, you could do that, too. The list went on. And the never-ending coffee mess was free and available all day long.

After a considerable amount of time had elapsed, I had lunch at a fellow worker's house, an ex-submariner, John Huszai. His wife asked me about caring for the children, and I told her that my biggest problem was with evening meals because preparation started only after I got home. Consequently, meals were always later than desired. John's wife, Mary, disappeared for a while, and, when she reappeared, she was carrying a box containing a brand-new Crockpot. She and John presented this to me and said, "This will solve a lot of your evening-meal problems." John and Mary had been in the habit of taking advantage of attending presentations about time shares or a new condo complex, after which they would receive a gift. They would plan an entire weekend hearing one presentation after another. They never bought or invested in anything, but they collected prize after prize. I became the proud recipient of one of the dozen or so Crockpots Mary and John had collected. Their prize collection included TVs, microwaves, blenders, and even a canoe!

After a pointer or two, I soon understood that Mary had given me a gem of a problem-solving device. The first time I used the Crockpot was to cook a venison roast that I had on hand. I literally stuffed the Crockpot with the roast, celery, carrots, onion, and potato, and filled the pot with water. After adding salt and pepper, I put the lid on and set the timer for eight hours. The kids and I went on with our daily activities, and, at the end of the day, when we all entered the house together, the most wonderful aroma of home cooking was permeating throughout the house.

I had completely forgotten about the Crockpot. I was instantly pissed and upset because my mind went to thinking that my ex-wife had somehow found us and gotten into the house and was cooking a meal for us. I was ready to confront this woman with my wrath, and I stormed into the kitchen, only to find it empty except for this wonderful thing on my kitchen counter, called a Crockpot—the dream and answer to my evening-meal dilemma.

## A Big Change Is About to Unfold

Time went on, and we all adjusted to our new way of life and routine quite well. One night the phone rang, and to my surprise, it was a representative of the U.S. Navy stationed at BUPERS (Bureau of Personnel). The rep informed me that a long list of officials had examined the circumstances of my seemingly impromptu departure. They now wanted to see if there was any way I could be induced into coming back into the Navy! After a lengthy discussion, I told him about the suggestion by a CO that I put my children in an orphanage and the chaplain story. He then told me about a friend of mine, Howard Slusser. Howard was a colorful character, to say the least, and a friend and a comrade. This old sonarman chief dedicated himself to coaching kids at Menriv Military Housing Complex. It seems one night he was talking to one of his volunteer coaches, and he mentioned my story. This volunteer coach was Admiral Pietsch. When he heard the story (my story), he investigated, and wanted to make amends. And now this rep from BUPERS was making the sales pitch to induce me to come back to the submarine Navy—with tons of incentives.

Explaining that my position was not complex—my main objective was to keep the family whole, safe, and sound—he assured me that the way I was treated in the past was being dealt with. Negotiations started in earnest. The outcome was that, if I agreed, I would go back to the FBMSTC and continue my duties as an instructor for an extended period of time and then transfer to a submarine Tender *USS Canopus* AS 34 after it entered the shipyard at Charleston, South Carolina. At the completion of the *Canopus*'s refit and overhaul, I would then *cross deck* to the *USS Simon Lake* AS 33, which would be entering Charleston Naval Shipyard upon the exiting of the *USS Canopus*. This was a deal I could not refuse. I would be able to—first and foremost—keep my family together and go back to the submarine Navy—and to the position of instructor that I loved.

The timing could not have been better. VITRO was going through some reconfiguration that would include me having to make many trips away from home. The money would be good for the inconvenience, but time away from home would not be tolerable to me. So, with my resignation submitted and all administrative tasks accomplished, there we were, our little band of nomads, making another pilgrimage and an exciting move back to Charleston, South Carolina—to all things familiar, warm, and wonderful to me and my children.

Before leaving our home in Maryland, our Hannibal Grove homeowners association held a going-away party for us. It was an event we would never forget. At that event, a request was made that I outline what I would be doing by rejoining the submarine Navy. The night extended long into the wee hours

## Phase Two of My Naval Career

as I told story after story about my experiences and exploits. After that night, I should have realized that the birth of this book probably started then—in a community meeting hall in Hannibal Grove, Columbia, Maryland.

Our trip back to Charleston was exciting. We stopped and saw some new sights that we'd missed before, but my crew was eager to get back and reunite with old friends and acquaintances. We chose a home not too far from my ex-wife to make it easier for visiting purposes—visits that never occurred; she had zero contact with her children. And that is how it has remained to this day.

The first day back at FBMSTC, I was met with an honor guard of old friends and instructors at the front entrance. A lot of laughs and welcome-back comments flowed back and forth. Following an extended welcome-party atmosphere, I had an invitation to meet with the new CO of the training center. He had replaced the previous CO—the one who recommended the orphanage for my kids. The new CO was Captain Richardson, and his focus was the mission of the training center—more specifically, the instructors. As he stated, more than once, we were the most vital ingredient.

When I finally arrived at my office, my desk was decorated like a Mardi Gras float, and it included a mock ticket back to VITRO. They were sick of me already! We laughed, and I felt such a strong feeling of love and respect. The whole experience of leaving the service and re-enlisting was a true lesson in life—and proof that the grass ain't always greener on the other side. My children and I were back where we should be—safe and happy.

And I was proudly back in uniform. I was most proud of my United States Naval Instructor's Badge on my chest. Out of all of the military decorations I earned, the instructor badge came in second only to my Submarine Dolphins. It has just occurred to me that I have failed to mention the importance of the Submarine Dolphins pin and emblem. Now that this book is coming to an end, I want to stress what this piece of jewelry and emblem means to me and my fellow submariners. The Dolphins pin is given to each submariner after completing qualifications while on patrol on an active submarine. I was given my Dolphins during my first patrol.

First of all, you have to understand that, to be presented with this piece of military jewelry, you must run a gauntlet of acquiring (and not easily acquired) knowledge of a very complicated nuclear submarine. This includes all electricals, electronics, hydraulics, pneumatics, and ballast plumbing, as well as an understanding of all of the weapons onboard, conventional and nuclear. You and your fellow sub mates have to team up and help one another to fully comprehend the complexities and the correct usage of every component onboard. And then you get tested, and sometimes (many times) you get rejected, and you have to start over again. Many sleepless nights and many bouts of frustration are experienced until the months (sometimes a year plus) finally culminate in your final testing and inquiry. This process could take days, but when you finally have passed the review of the final onboard group of experts (qualified senior submariners), you are welcomed to the exclusive club of "Qualified in Submarines."

## Phase Two of My Naval Career

Each week there is always someone celebrating this achievement, and the Captain is the one who performs the pinning ceremony. It is when you finally realize that you have accomplished a monumental feat. This is a bigger deal than most people will comprehend initially. Onboard a sub, you might be the only one in a particular part of the sub and responsible for everything in that area. When something goes wrong, it might be life or death for every man onboard. With your acquired knowledge, you can and will perform steps that will save the submarine and all onboard. So, excuse me if I belabor the point.

When I see Dolphins on the chest of a submariner on the news or in a movie, I always have a humbling and emotional response. I wear a denim jacket with a huge set of dolphins embossed on the back, and I wear it with cocky pride. I have gotten wonderful compliments from the few who recognize and understand what the emblem stands for.

As I wax on about the importance of the Dolphins pin and emblem, I want to mention all of the present and past service members of all branches of the services. In today's present-day political climate, I believe our entire armed services are ignored and demeaned. So, I ask you all to look at the service members you come in contact with and not ignore them. Look at their insignias and their decorations, and realize each decoration marks an accomplishment that they had to sacrifice time and effort in order to get and that it all happened separated from their loved ones. All of those decorations represent learned and practiced skills to keep America free. You, my friends, should take the time and acknowledge every serviceman you come in contact with.

And this is the last comment I will make on this. For every service member you see, remember there are thousands of soldiers, sailors, Marines, and Air Force members overseas assuring your freedom. And I have to mention, there are also hundreds of nuclear submariners submerged, as we speak, on patrol, keeping our adversaries constantly aware that, if they choose to do something hostile or stupid, we will respond and crush them.

My last years in the Navy were marked with many great events. There were some low points, to be sure, but the good outweighed the bad exponentially.

## My Retirement Ceremony

After a whole lot of experiences both good and not so good, the day had arrived—the day of my retirement ceremony, and the day I was to put my United States Nuclear Submarine career into mothballs. This was the final day I would wear my full-dress uniform and assemble with my peers.

In my mind, I downplayed the whole thing a bit and did not think that a lot of hoopla was necessary. But then, as I stood on the stage, in the auditorium of the Fleet Ballistic Missile Submarine Training Center, where I enjoyed many important events—some directed at me and many directed to esteemed colleagues and other dignitaries—it hit me. This *was* a big deal. That day, the auditorium was filled to the brim with people with whom I'd come into contact over my many years of service, as

## Phase Two of My Naval Career

well as past COs (commanding officers), other officers, fellow instructors, many students whom I had the privilege to teach, my civilian friends, and especially my family.

The festivities were humbling, and they brought tears to my eyes throughout the entire event. One of my COs, Captain Hale, took the stage and summed up my career by listing all of the exploits I had been part of, such as the hundreds of thousands of miles I had traveled underwater, and the number of days submerged, which added up to almost three full years of submerged time. He also added to the list things like how many gallons of water the Navy wasted on me to shower and the number of chickens killed to feed me. The list went on and on, and the crowd told other stories and exposed stats of my days as a submariner. There were many good laughs, and we all had a great time.

My retirement ceremony actually turned into a ROAST. It was all fun, but I have to admit that, when I heard about the submerged time, it kind of shook me and woke me up. But truth to tell, I would do it all over again. And to top it all off, I exited the FBMSTC for the last time under a gauntlet of fellow instructors with drawn swords on high while the Navy hymn played in the background. That was an emotional moment, to be sure.

After the ceremony was over, it took five of my colleagues and family members to carry the awards, gifts, and tributes bestowed on me to our cars. My retirement was a moment in time that I cannot, and never will, forget. When the ceremony ended, the Chiefs' Club was the next stop for all of us, and the festivities continued with the introduction of high-octane liquid refreshments. The drinks flowed, and a good time was had by all. Hangovers were plenty the next day.

Amidst all of this celebrating, I told a group of friends that maybe I should call off my retirement and stick around a bit longer. That suggestion on my part was rejected by my old friends, and I was told that I had worn out my welcome and they sent me a hearty "Good Riddance." There were laughs, hugs, salutes, and plenty of tears all around, and that's when it hit me. I had to get used to the fact that an era was truly over and that the first day of the rest of my life as a retired service member was about to begin.

Although the book is a snapshot of (and nowhere near a complete compilation of all of my experiences onboard or building subs), I have recreated the service flow of all of the commands at which I was stationed, both shore and sea duty, so that you may get a better idea of the sequence of events in which I took part in the very secretive and silent world of the *silent service*. The timeline of my Naval career follows.

Phase Two of My Naval Career

# Timeline of My Naval Career

Navy Recruit Training
Great Lakes, Illinois
February 1962–May '62

AUW School
Key West, Florida
June '62–August '62

Navy Sub School
New London, Connecticut
September '62–October '62

Missile Launcher School
Dam Neck, Virginia
November '62–February '63

*USS Nathan Hale*
SSBN 623G
March '63–September '65

*USS George C. Marshall*
SSBN 654G
October '65–March '69

*USS Entemedor*
SS 340
April '69–October '69

Poseidon Missile School
Dam Neck, Virginia
November '69–December '69

*USS John C. Calhoun*
SSBN630 G
January '70–December '70

Instructor School
Norfolk, Virginia
January '73–February '73

FBMSTC
Charleston, South Carolina
March '73–February '73

*USS James K. Polk*
SSBN 645B
March '76–November '76

*USS Canopus*
AS—34
June '76–November '76

*USS Simon Lake*
AS—33
December '76–December '76

*USS George Bancroft*
SSBN 643B
January '79–April '80

FBMSTC
Charleston, South Carolina
May '80–October '83

# C. Civilian Life

The years that followed were years filled with different kinds of experiences, to be sure, as I carried on as a civilian. I lived my life as best I could, but the memories of my days at sea and the life I led as a submariner remained with me always. I became an entrepreneur and a real estate broker, and I spent many successful years renovating homes for resale, i.e., flipping houses. And I continued to try to make the most of my wretched life at home, until my second wife passed away. And then a miracle happened!

There is a time when the stories have to stop, and my book has to be brought to an end. And that time is now. In the beginning, I alluded to a surprise that would come sometime later in my book. Well, excitedly, it is my joy to tell you this amazing story.

Real Stories from a Nuclear Submariner

## Story: Incredulous

Several years after my retirement from the U.S. Navy and after my second wife passed away, my daughter-in-law signed me up on an internet site called Facebook, and she tutored me on how to utilize it. The next day I turned on my computer and opened the Facebook app. The original purpose of my going on Facebook was to link up with old submarine buddies, but instead of finding anyone from my submarine life, only one name appeared—Ann Patavino Vincola. This was my high school sweetheart, the very one who had broken up with me and spurred on my immature behavior of quitting college and joining the Navy, which, of course, led to my joining the ranks as a nuclear submariner.

Let's get back to that fateful day. When I saw the name on my computer, I immediately stood up, and I was shaken to my core. After some pause, I sent a feeble message; "Are you the same Ann Patavino I went to high school with?" A couple of hours later, a reply finally arrived, "Of course, it's me. How are you?" I was ecstatic. The years of great memories came rushing out of the corners of my mind.

I thought I was being humorous by reminding her of our first date, but little did I know that my post on Facebook was such that everyone could read it. In that post, I recalled an occurrence on our first date. We went to a movie, and, upon exiting the theater, I realized my fly (zipper) was broken. I told Ann about my embarrassing dilemma, and we went around a corner for some privacy to attempt to fix it. Fumbling with my zipper, we had passers-by laughing and giggling. Ann's

## Phase Two of My Naval Career

response at that point was to give me her email address, so that we would have a more secure channel of communication.

Many many emails followed. Our reuniting was rapid. After learning that Ann was single, I was bound and determined that I wasn't going to let this opportunity pass me by. I informed her after our third day of reconnecting that the love light for her had only gone dim—it never went out. I told her that forty-eight years and three days later, I was still in love with her. Her answer was "Incredulous." We exchanged phone numbers, and our first phone call lasted three hours.

Of all of our parents, Ann's mother, Helen, was the only one still alive. Ann and her sister Emma were dining with their mom when Ann asked her, "Mom, do you remember Alan Votta?" Her reply was magic to my ears, "You mean the man I thought you were going to marry!" Now this was coming from a ninety-four-year-old woman. And then Emmie, noticeably disturbed, said, "You took Alan away from Mom, and Dad, and you took him away from me, too."

Time marched on, and we finally met face-to-face. Our long-delayed reunion had come to pass—as fate would have it. And before the year was over, our wedding was being planned. Our wedding was held in Charleston, South Carolina, with eleven of our fellow high school classmates attending, among all our other guests. It was a wonderful occasion. Our fiftieth high school reunion was coming up the following year, so some of our wedding guests became the nucleus of the committee to put that reunion together. The reunion was a huge success, and those connections continue to this day.

*Real Stories from a Nuclear Submariner*

All of what I have spouted here is covered in a book that my wife wrote. The title is *Reunited: When the Past Becomes a Present*. We have been happily married for more than eleven years now. We are still in love with life and with one another in this paradise called Sarasota, Florida.

—⚓—

So, as I end my book, it is my hope that I have offered some inspiration and some humor, but, above all, that I have expressed my gratitude to the United States Submarine Service, of which I was a proud member.

Putting pen to paper and writing this book has been such a valued experience for me, not only because it refreshed my memory of some long-forgotten episodes, but it gave me a greater sense of accomplishment and pride in my Navy career. As we were finishing up on this overwhelming activity and task and beginning to search for photos, I was amazed at what I found. I discovered so many resources and a bountiful quantity of videos about submarines and submarine life in both artwork and in videos. Therefore, if you have been bitten by the bug of wanting to know more about this *arsenal for peace*, there is plenty out there to satisfy you.

I have now viewed many videos, especially older ones that depict my era aboard submarines. Many moments are in lockstep with my words, and, in a clip or two, I recognized shipmates and acquaintances, and I know that I am in some of those shots myself. These videos and photos have reminded me that I possibly took for granted what I had done and of what

## Phase Two of My Naval Career

I was a part. Yes, I downplayed what my fellow submariners accomplished and what the thousands of young studs who are on patrol today are doing for us now.

I can only hope that you are curious enough to take advantage of the goldmine of information that YouTube can provide about submarines!

# Part Five

# Final Stories

Ah, you thought I was finished with my little book and telling my stories. Well, I can't help myself. There are a few additional thoughts that have come to my mind as I complete the telling of my adventures as a submariner, and they are worth including. It has been amazing to me how my brain has been awakened to so many of these memories as I pursued this writing activity. In the construction of a book, after the book has come to an official end, a last-minute thought or story can be added, and it does not necessarily have to relate to the book content. This is called the *Afterword,* but in the tradition of this author, I prefer to refer to it as the *Afterfart*! Here goes.

# A. USS Thresher SSN 593

While I was stationed at the United States Naval Shipyard in Portsmouth, New Hampshire, I had an encounter with a marine/Naval architect. I was sent to the shipyard on a temporary assignment to help in the co-ordination to overhaul an old World War II submarine, the *USS Entemedore* SS 340 boat.

The overhaul was very delicate and had to be handled accurately and precisely because this sub was going to be a gift to the nation of Iran. Yes, it was a different day insofar as our relationship with that country was concerned. So, I was there with other expert submarine overhaulers to make sure the sub was going to be transferred in tip-top condition. That meant we had to talk to and rub shoulders with some of the most brilliant minds in the design-engineering department of the shipyard. Some of these gentlemen actually were very instrumental and deeply involved in the design and construction of the *USS Thresher*, which had sunk some five or six years before. One of the marine architects, whose nickname was "Rickover," because he and Admiral Rickover had a special engineering relationship. His real name is lost to history and time, but he was one very savvy and smart guy.

While there, he and I would from time to time meet up and have a beer or two and "talk shop." On one occasion, he remarked to me, "Do you want to know why the *Thresher* really sank?!?!" Boy, oh boy, did he have my attention! He went on to tell me that, among many theories, the one he was about to tell me was the one you could take to the bank and bet on for sure!

So here goes the theory. Onboard all submarines, there are many valves attached to the hull below the deck plates in the area called "the bilge." There are bilges that accumulate various quantities of water on purpose and by design that are routinely pumped out. The valves are immersed from time to time. These valves were electro/hydraulically operated, and occasionally the electrical hookups would fail due to flooded electrical connections. Therefore, a design modification was devised and installed on the *Thresher,* which consisted of building up the hull mounting base to a height to keep the water from infiltrating the electrical components of the remote operating capability. These new raised valve mounting bases were given an affectionate name of *The Ant Hills.* Picture a plant stand eight inches to twelve inches tall, and then picture a hunk of HY80 steel eight inches to twelve inches tall with an electro/hydraulic valve on top.

My friend was very somber when he relayed this story to me. He went on to say that he fought the design but that he had been politely overridden by unnamed persons. He continued to reveal that the welding practice at the time would not ensure a full and total adhesion to the hull. So, according to his theory, when the *Thresher* went to test depth, he felt that one of these *Ant Hills* carried away, and the extreme pressurized spray and flood of water rapidly crippled the sub in mere minutes, leading to its demise.

His last remarks to me were that he had been haunted by his beliefs and theory and that he knew all of the shipyard reps who were riders onboard as well as a number of the crew members. His final remark to me on the subject was, "Don't get me into trouble by relating or telling this story!" Rickover Rick and I continued to get together from time to time, but we never talked about the *Thresher* again. And this is the first time I have thought about this encounter...or spoken of it, in fifty-plus years!

# B. THE HUNLEY

I would be remiss if I did not mention the *Hunley* at all in my little book. The significance of the part that the *Hunley* played in the growth of submarines, in general, cannot be minimized, in my opinion. *The Hunley* was the first attempt at building an underwater vessel.

I was privileged to be part of the ceremony of the proper burial for the crew of the *Hunley*, the Civil War icon, after it was located and raised from the harbor in Charleston, South Carolina. *The Hunley* was the first submarine to sink a ship in time of war—the *USS Housatonic*. Early in the construction of the *Hunley*, with its first crew onboard, the *Hunley* tried to test submergence next to the pier; however, the submersible took on a torrent of water and sank, drowning the first crew of the submarine. After that tragedy, a second crew was also lost due to unknown flooding circumstances, following the sinking of the *Housatonic*.

The burial for the second crew of the *Hunley*, which I attended, was held at the Magnolia Cemetery in Charleston, South Carolina—a place everyone should visit, not only because it is the final resting place for the two crews of the *Hunley*, but for all of its historical significance. The first crew of the *Hunley* is buried in another section of the cemetery. I felt so privileged to be there on that day.

The *Hunley* remains an important symbol in the infancy of submarine development.

# C. Strange Occurrences or Stranger Encounters

This is a topic that will make you wonder and make you shake your head, but it is in its entirety all true. Over the years I have on countless occasions cause to re-think some of the exploits I have had, and I realized that many of these moments were tied to my submarine comrades and acquaintances, like Engineman 1st class Jimmy Buffern, who could strip down any diesel engine onboard any submarine and re-assemble it in the dark or in battle. Jimmy died in the shears (where the topside lookouts would scan the horizon for visual contacts) of the *USS Clamagore* SS 343 and fell to the deck. It was discovered later that he had suffered a burst brain aneurism. And then there was Jimmy Augustus Snyder, who died onboard the *USS Nathan Hale* SSBN 623G, whom you read about earlier in this book. Let me add another name—Augustus G. Hootmacher.

*Real Stories from a Nuclear Submariner*

Years after retiring from the Submarine Navy, when I was renovating houses for resale, I bought an old house, a Sears Roebuck Kit House (look that up!) It was originally purchased and constructed by Augustus G. Hootmacher in 1927 or 1928. As I was working in the attic and was in need of a knife, I said out loud, "Mr. Hootmacher, I need a knife." Immediately afterward, I felt a cold hand on my head pushing my face to the left…as I then stared at an old knife lying within my reach. Shaken a little, I simply said, "Thank you, Mr. Hootmacher." True story. This ain't no bullshit! This is only one example of *visits* I have had from deceased individuals and the reason I mention it here.

Several years after that incident, I volunteered to chaperone my grandson's sixth-grade class on a field trip to Patriot's Point (Maritime Museum) in Mount Pleasant, South Carolina. The weather was terrible that day, and, because it was midweek, there were no other tourists around. The World War II Submarine *USS Clamagore* SS 343 boat was a main attraction, along with the *USS Yorktown* CV10/CVA aircraft carrier.

Our small group went down a very long pier to the *Clamagore*. Yes, it was the very submarine that Jimmy Buffern was stationed on and where he lost his life, and the submarine was now a museum attraction. We were directed to the forward Torpedo Room hatch area to climb down to start the tour, and then we were to exit from the After Torpedo Room hatch to keep large crowds moving. The other chaperones and I kept the children in order, and we eventually entered the After Battery Compartment, the entire area of which had been gutted and was now a gallery dedicated to all of the subs

## Final Stories

sunk in World War II. A plaque for each submarine with all of the crewmembers' names filled the compartment.

I lingered and realized there was a gentleman standing nearby reading one of the plaques. The children proceeded aft, and this gentleman and I were alone. He was wearing an old set of Navy bell-bottom trousers and a blue chambre shirt. Retired submariners volunteered to visit the sub and served as tour guides and also did some maintenance work when necessary, so this man didn't seem out of place to me. However, when he addressed me, his voice sounded a little emotional and a little strange. He then turned directly to me and said, "I knew a lot of these men." I noticed the name "Snyder" stenciled above his left-side shirt pocket. He turned, and then I had to get along and do a little chaperoning. I felt like I knew this man. It bothered me, but I couldn't place the face.

We exited the sub and took the gangway to the long, empty pier and assembled at the end in an enclosed area to have lunch. Consequently, anyone leaving the pier and dock area had to come through us to exit. I kept staring down the long pier at the sub. The museum staff had prepared three different lectures for us, consuming a lot of time. During all of this time, I monitored the sub, keeping a watchful eye out for my gentleman friend, whom I had left behind reading the plaques. He never appeared, and I had this weird feeling that I had been in the company of another apparition—like Mr. Hootmacher. At one point in time, I excused myself as the next lecture began, and I headed down the long pier and entered the sub again. This time I entered from the After Torpedo Room, going in reverse, not wanting to miss anybody exiting the sub as I worked my way from aft to forward. I checked every nook and cranny, especially the museum area and After Battery, and proceeded to the Forward Torpedo Room, and then exited the sub. I might add that, on a sub, there is absolutely no other place one could hide.

Quickly looking down the pier and topside on the sub, there was no one to be seen. It was such a cold, rainy, and dismal day, and now it had a strange element added…for me at least. Where did my gentleman friend in the old Navy dungarees with the name of "Snyder" disappear to? Then it hit me like a ton of bricks. I suddenly realized this gentleman looked like my old friend Jimmy Buffern (deceased) wearing a shirt with the name "Snyder" (Jimmy Snyder—deceased). Now bring in Mr. Augustus G. Hootmacher.

This was all I could see. Do you see the name "Jimmy"? Do you see "Augustus"? And do you see "Snyder"? All three are deceased, and two of the three have made contact with me. That's why I believe that Jimmy did appear to me while I was writing about him in my book.

I have been visited by my mother and my wife's father, and I have had some other unexplainable happenings occur in my life. I am willing and waiting for more to come! Strange encounters, indeed.

# D. A Submarine Sailor Walked into a Bar...

*N*ow this last bit is my attempt at being funny and ending this diatribe with humor. I found this piece in some Naval magazine years ago, and, since the submariner spelled out so much of what I had experienced, I found it pretty hilarious. Of course, I have tried to use this story as a joke during several gatherings with friends. Somehow I usually mess it up, and the punch line falls flat—or so my wife says! It goes over much better in the written form. Therefore, I am going to simply re-write this little ditty for you.

*An old Submarine sailor walked into a bar. As he sat sipping his drink, a young, good-looking woman sat down next to him. She turned to the old guy and saw the dolphins on his ball cap and the baseball warm-up jacket he was wearing, and asked, "Are you a real Submarine sailor?" He replied, "Well, my father, two brothers, and a third cousin were on the 'boats.' I've* spent my whole life, riding 'boats.' Snorkeling, deep dives, Diesel Boats, Nuclear Power, Med Runs, Northern Runs, Deterrent Missile Patrols, Arctic Runs, SPECOPS, WESTPACs, runs to the Caribbean, Halifax Faslane, Holy Loch, Rota, Naples, 2 day runs, Blue Crew, Gold Crew, the other crew, 90-day patrols, 6-month deployments, been through the "ditch," across the equator, under the ice, and up to the pole. Pearl, Yokosuka, Guam, La Madd, Fort Lauderdale, San Juan, tracked ruskies, dodged P-3s, been depth charged, torpedoed, tracked with Active Sonar, detected by SOSUS, built them, decommissioned them, overhauled them, recommissioned them, been a Blue Nose, Sheliback, Blown from test depth, gone emergency deep, rode Tridents, 688s, 637s, 594s, Skipjack and Franklin class, drug runs, liquor runs, crazy Ivans, been in trail, used a Steinke hood, been through the tower, dodged Russian air power, fought flooding, fires, reactor scrams, stood watch on the Ballast Control Panel, Ship's Control Panel, Electric Control Panel, Garbage Disposal Unit and Trash Disposal Unit. I got dolphins, a combat patrol pin, deterrent patrol pin and "Diesel Boats Forever" tattooed on my chest, THRESHER on my left arm, SCORPION on my right arm, Missiles on my back, and twin counter rotating screw on my ass. I've drunk beer at the Horse and Cow, scotch at Highland Mary's in Dunoon, wine in Naples, puked at Beaman's Center in Pearl, ate Chili at the SUBVETS, drank whiskey at Rosie's in Groton, and I ain't missed a Submarine Ball since 1956, so I guess I am a Submarine sailor."

She said, "I'm a lesbian. I spend my whole day thinking about women. As soon as I get up in the morning, I think about women. When I shower, I think about women. When I watch

*TV, I think about women. I even think about women when I eat. It seems that everything makes me think about women.*

*The two sat sipping their drinks in silence. A little later, a man sat down on the other side of the old Submariner, noticed his ball cap, and jacket and said, "You must be a Submariner!"*

*The old boy replies: "Well, I always thought I was, but I just found out I'm a lesbian."*

*Any more Bubbleheads out there?*

And, so my friends, I leave you with that. And THAT AIN'T NO BULLSHIT! Over and out.

# About the Author

After serving for more than twenty-three years, conducting sixteen patrols, and then retiring from the United States Nuclear Submarine Force, Mr. Votta joined the civilian world in various entrepreneurial capacities. At one point, he was the owner of a pawn shop, after which he ventured into real estate as a broker and an investor, renovating many properties for resale. Later he was a successful owner/operator of a wallpaper/window blind/decorating business. He has always had a keen interest in antiques and collectibles, and in travel, especially to Italy, where he and his wife hold dual citizenship. Currently Mr. Votta enjoys full retirement in Sarasota, Florida, with his wife, Ann.

www.ingramcontent.com/pod-product-compliance
Lightning Source LLC
Chambersburg PA
CBHW062243300426
44110CB00034B/1301